新能源汽车专业系列教材

新能源汽车专业英语

主　编　宋进桂　徐永亮
副主编　刘本超　彭朝晖　汤少岩
参　编　贺翠华　吕瑞霞　张黎黎

本书共分9章，内容包括新能源汽车的发展和技术概况、电动汽车主要组成部分（动力电池、牵引电机和控制器、传动系统）的结构原理与维护、典型电动汽车车型介绍、电动汽车故障诊断与维护、电动汽车设计、燃料电池汽车构造与原理，以及压缩天然气-汽油双燃料汽车构造与维护，通过相关内容的介绍，使读者对紧贴技术发展的新能源汽车专业英语知识有更全面的了解。附录收集了丰田普锐斯混合动力控制系统故障诊断数据、常用汽车英语缩写与含义、常用汽车专业术语和传统汽车结构图解英中对照。书中每节内容包括课文、生词表、短语术语表，每章后有疑难句分析注解。

本书可作为应用型本科车辆工程专业及高职高专、新能源汽车专业及其他汽车类专业的"新能源汽车专业英语"课程教材，也可作为企业培训教材或汽车行业从业人员的自学教材。

为方便教学，本书配套有多媒体课件，提供所有课文的参考译文，选用本书作为教材的教师可从机械工业出版社教育服务网（www.cmpedu.com）免费下载，或发送邮件至13744491@qq.com获取。

图书在版编目（CIP）数据

新能源汽车专业英语／宋进桂，徐永亮主编．—北京：
机械工业出版社，2020.7（2025.6重印）
新能源汽车专业系列教材
ISBN 978-7-111-66097-2

Ⅰ.①新… Ⅱ.①宋… ②徐… Ⅲ.①新能源-汽车工程-英语-高等职业教育-教材 Ⅳ.①U469.7

中国版本图书馆CIP数据核字（2020）第124775号

机械工业出版社（北京市百万庄大街22号　邮政编码100037）
策划编辑：赵海青　　　责任编辑：赵海青　王　婕
责任校对：丁　锋　　　责任印制：李　昂
涿州市京南印刷厂印刷
2025年6月第1版第10次印刷
184mm×260mm · 12印张 · 245千字
标准书号：ISBN 978-7-111-66097-2
定价：45.00元

电话服务　　　　　　　网络服务
客服电话：010-88361066　机　工　官　网：www.cmpbook.com
　　　　　010-88379833　机　工　官　博：weibo.com/cmp1952
　　　　　010-68326294　金　书　网：www.golden-book.com
封底无防伪标均为盗版　机工教育服务网：www.cmpedu.com

前 言

汽车的普及给人类带来了极大的方便，但同时也带来了许多烦恼——传统能源的大量消耗以及大量有害物质的排放。为此，汽车制造商正在研究和制造替代传统能源汽车的新能源汽车，世界各大汽车公司也都拥有自己的油-电混合动力汽车和纯电动汽车车型或品牌。在有影响力的车展上，混合动力汽车和纯电动汽车正在博得更多的关注，许多国家也都提出了停售传统燃料汽车的最后时限，汽车能源的大变革时代正在到来。

目前，世界各大汽车商均有混合动力车型或纯电动车型在华销售，我国在纯电动汽车的研发和生产方面也已经处于世界领先地位。混合动力电动汽车和纯电动汽车所占的比例在迅速提高。汽车研发、设计、生产、销售和售后服务各个领域对新能源汽车给予了更多的重视，许多高等院校设置了新能源汽车专业或相关课程。为满足"新能源汽车专业英语"课程教学的需要，我们编写了本书。

本书图文并茂，通俗易懂。每篇课文的后面附有生词表和短语术语表，每章后都有疑难句的分析注解（NOTES）。

本书总学时数建议为28～36，各章建议学时见下表，各校可以根据实际情况进行调整。

章序	英文章名	中文章名	建议学时
1	Overview of the New Energy Vehicles	新能源汽车概述	2～4
2	Power Batteries of EVs	电动汽车动力电池	4～6
3	Traction Motors and Controllers	牵引电机与控制器	4
4	Transmission Systems	传动系统	4～6
5	Brief Description to Some Typical EVs	典型电动汽车简介	4
6	Trouble Diagnosis and Service of Electric Vehicles	电动汽车故障诊断与维护	4
7	Design Aspects of Electric Vehicles	电动汽车设计概略	2～4
8	Fuel Cell Powered Vehicles	燃料电池汽车	2
9	CNG-Gasoline Dual-fuel Vehicles	压缩天然气—汽油双燃料汽车	2

本书由鲁东大学宋进桂、烟台汽车工程职业学院徐永亮担任主编；山东交通职业学院刘本超、潇湘职业学院彭朝晖、烟台汽车工程职业学院汤少岩担任副主编；烟台汽车工程职业学院贺翠华、吕瑞霞、张黎黎参与了本书的编写工作。具体分工如下：彭朝晖编写第1章和附录B；宋进桂编写第2、3章；徐永亮编写第4章和附录E；汤少岩编写第5章；刘本超编写第6章和附录A；贺翠华编写第7章和附录C；张黎黎编写第8章；吕瑞霞编写第9章和附录D。本书在编写过程中得到了编者所在学校和老师的大力支持。学校老师们对本书的编写提出了许多宝贵的建议，提供了部分参考资料，编者在此深表谢意。

由于编者专业水平有限，本书难免会存在疏漏和不当之处，敬请读者给予批评指正。

编 者

目 录

前言

Chapter 1
Overview of the New Energy Vehicles　新能源汽车概述

1.1　The Development of Electric Vehicles 电动汽车的发展 …………………… 001
1.2　Overview of Alternative Fuel Vehicles 替代燃料汽车概述 ………………… 005
1.3　Classifications of Electric Vehicles 电动汽车的分类 …………………………… 008

Chapter 2
Power Batteries of EVs　电动汽车动力电池

2.1　Basic Terminology and Types of Power Batteries 动力电池的基本术语和类型 …… 013
2.2　Battery Construction and Principle 电池结构与原理 …………………………… 017
2.3　Battery Management and Cooling Systems 电池管理与冷却系统 …………… 025
2.4　Battery Charging Technology 电池充电技术 …………………………………… 028
2.5　Service and Testing 维护与测试 ……………………………………………… 030

Chapter 3
Traction Motors and Controllers　牵引电机与控制器

3.1　Types of Traction Motors 牵引电机的类型 …………………………………… 036
3.2　Construction and Principle 结构与原理 ………………………………………… 038
3.3　Motor Control System (controllers) 电机控制系统 …………………………… 044
3.4　Service and Testing 维护与测试 ……………………………………………… 048

Chapter 4

Transmission Systems 传动系统

4.1　Classification of Hybrid Drive 混合动力的分类 ………………………………… 050

4.2　Passenger Car Hybrid Drive 乘用车混合动力传动系统 ……………………… 054

Chapter 5

Brief Description to Some Typical EVs 典型电动汽车简介

5.1　Fuel Efficiency Measures 燃料经济性测量 …………………………………… 070

5.2　Some Typical BEVs 典型纯电动汽车 …………………………………………… 072

5.3　Some Typical HEVs 典型混合动力汽车 ………………………………………… 074

Chapter 6

Trouble Diagnosis and Service of Electric Vehicles 电动汽车故障诊断与维护

6.1　General Trouble Diagnosis Procedure and Safety Equipments 一般故障诊断程序和安全设备 ……………………………………………………………………………… 085

6.2　Toyota Prius Hybrid Trouble Diagnosis 丰田普锐斯混合动力汽车故障诊断 …… 089

Chapter 7

Design Aspects of Electric Vehicles 电动汽车设计概略

7.1　Layout of Electric Vehicle Drives 电动汽车传动布置 ………………………… 099

7.2　Design Criteria of Batteries 蓄电池设计原则 ………………………………… 102

7.3　Optimization Techniques - Mathematical Modeling 优化技术-数学建模 ……… 105

Chapter 8

Fuel Cell Powered Vehicles 燃料电池汽车

8.1　Overview of Fuel Cell Technology 燃料电池技术概述 ………………………… 110

8.2　Fuel Cell Electric Vehicle (FCEV) and Fuel Cell Hybrid Electric Vehicle (FCHEV) 燃料电池电动汽车(FCEV)与燃料电池混合动力汽车(FCHEV) ……………… 115

Chapter 9
CNG-Gasoline Dual-fuel Vehicles 压缩天然气-汽油双燃料汽车

9.1 Natural Gas Nature and Features 天然气的性质与特点……………………………… 119
9.2 Construction of CNG-Gasoline Dual-fuel Vehicle CNG-汽油双燃料汽车的构造 … 120
9.3 Service Notes 维护提示…………………………………………………………… 123

附 录

附录 A 丰田普锐斯混合动力控制系统故障诊断数据……………………………… 124
附录 B 常用汽车英语缩写与含义…………………………………………………… 141
附录 C 常用汽车专业术语…………………………………………………………… 150
附录 D 词汇总表（英中对照）……………………………………………………… 160
附录 E 传统汽车结构图解…………………………………………………………… 171

参考文献 …………………………………………………………………………… 184

Chapter 1

Overview of the New Energy Vehicles
新能源汽车概述

1.1 The Development of Electric Vehicles
电动汽车的发展

The early days (1890 – 1930): The golden age

Practical and more successful electric road vehicles were invented by both American Thomas Davenport and Scotsman Robert Davidson around 1842.

France and Great Britain were the first nations to support the widespread development of electric vehicles in the late 1800s. In 1899, a Belgian built electric racing car called "La Jamais Contente" set a world record for land speed — 68 mph.

In 1901, Ferdinand Porsche developed the Lohner-Porsche Mixte Hybrid, the first gasoline-electric hybrid automobile in the world. It was originally an electric-powered vehicle and then a gasoline engine was added to recharge the battery. Another hybrid car that used both a gasoline engine and an electric motor to power the vehicle was built by Woods Motor Company of Chicago in 1916, Illinois, and was called the "Woods Dual Power".

The early electric vehicles, such as the 1902 Wood's Phaeton (Figure 1.1), were little more than electrified horseless carriages. The Phaeton had a range of 18 miles, a top speed of 14 mph and cost $2000.

The years 1899 and 1900 were the high point of electric cars in America, as they outsold all other types of cars. While basic electric cars cost under $1000, most early electric vehicles were ornate. They had fancy interiors, with expensive materials, and averaged $3000 by 1910. Electric vehicles enjoyed success into the 1920s with production peaking in 1912.

Figure 1.1 1902 Wood's Phaeton

The middle years (1930 – 1990): Falling into a depression

The decline of the electric vehicle was brought about by several major developments, such as a better system of roads in America by the 1920s, lower gasoline car price than electric cars due to the initiation of mass production of internal combustion engine vehicles by Henry Ford, the discovery of Texas crude oil and the invention of the electric starter in 1912 eliminating the need for the hand crank[*1].

Electric vehicles had all but disappeared by 1935. The years following until the 1960s were dead years for electric vehicle development and for use as personal transportation.

The 1970s when the oil crisis occurred saw a need for alternative fueled vehicles to reduce the dependency on imported foreign crude oil. Many manufactures were beginning the development of electric cars.

In the 1980s, crude oil was supplied substantially and its price was reduced. The pace of development of electric cars slowed down.

The recent years (1990 – 1998): Making a comeback

Several legislative and regulatory actions in the United States and worldwide have renewed electric vehicle development efforts. Primary among these is the U. S. 1990 Clean Air Act Amendment, the U. S. 1992 Energy Policy Act, and regulations issued by the California Air Resources Board (CARB). In addition to more stringent air emissions requirements and regulations requiring reductions in gasoline use, several states have issued Zero Emission Vehicle requirements.

The "Big Three" automobile manufacturers, and the U. S. Department of Energy, as well as a number of vehicle conversion companies are actively involved in electric vehicle development through the Partnership for a New Generation of Vehicles (PNGV). Electric conversions of familiar gasoline powered vehicles, as well as electric vehicles designed from the ground up, are now available that reach super highway speeds with ranges of 50 to 150 miles between recharging.

Ford and General Motors during 1998, made the Ranger, the EV1, and the S-10 pickup. During 1998 the Toyota RAV4 sport utility, the Honda EV Plus sedan, and the Chrysler EPIC minivan were also introduced. These vehicles were all equipped with advanced nickel metal hydride battery packs.

The current and future (Since 1998): Be still making progress

The hybrid electric vehicle did not become widely available until the release of the Toyota Prius in Japan in 1997, followed by the Honda Insight sold in the United States starting in 1999. Then in 2001, the first Toyota Prius (Figure 1.2) was introduced in the United States.

By 2010, there were several electric vehicles for sale although often in limited parts of the country and in limited numbers. Electric vehicles include the Tesla (Figure 1.3), Nissan Leaf, and Chevrolet Volt. Now, conventional automakers and some new companies sale mass-produced electric cars and hybrid cars.

Figure 1.2 2001 Toyota Prius

Figure 1.3 2008 Tesla Roadster

Hydrogen, Electric and Hybrid cars have been developed and demonstrated in several exhibitions. At the 2019 Frankfurt auto show Mercedes-Benz unveils the Vision EQS concept car. Its driving range is up to 400 miles (700 km). The 0 – 60 mph (97 km/h) run takes less than 4.5 s. The lithium-ion battery could be recharged to 80% capacity in less than 20 minutes.

Zero-emission vehicles using an electric powertrain system based on hydrogen fuel cells or purely battery electric systems that are fully competitive to conventional vehicles regarding performance and ease-of-use represent the ultimate target of the future strategy as shown in Figure 1.4[*2].

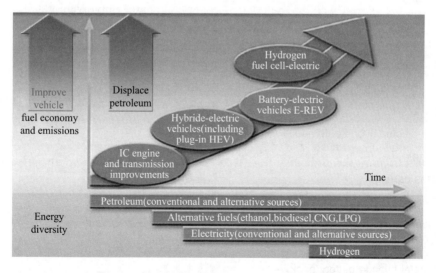

Figure 1.4 GM's advance propulsion strategy

New Words		
decline	[dɪˈklaɪn]	n. 下降；衰退
electrified	[ɪˈlektrɪfaɪd]	adj. 电气化的
fancy	[ˈfænsi]	adj. 精致的；豪华的
hybrid	[ˈhaɪbrɪd]	n. 杂交生成的生物体，混合物
initiation	[ɪˌnɪʃiˈeɪʃn]	n. 开始
minivan	[ˈmɪnɪvæn]	n. 微型厢式车
ornate	[ɔːˈneɪt]	adj. 装饰华丽的
outsold	[ˌaʊtˈsəʊld]	v. 比……卖得多
pickup	[ˈpɪkʌp]	n. 皮卡
range	[reɪndʒ]	n. 范围，射程，续驶里程
sedan	[sɪˈdæn]	n. 轿子，（四门）轿车
strategy	[ˈstrætədʒi]	n. 策略，战略
widespread	[ˈwaɪdspred]	adj. 分布广的，普遍的

Phrases and Technical Terms	
alternative fuel	替代燃料
E-REV	增程式电动汽车
CNG	压缩天然气
LPG	液化石油气
alternative fueled vehicle	替代燃料汽车
electric motor	电动机
electric starter	起动机
electric vehicle	电动汽车
electric-powered vehicle	电动汽车
from the ground up	从头开始
gasoline engine	汽油机
gasoline-electric hybrid automobile	油电混合动力汽车
hand crank	起动摇把
horseless carriage	无马的马车，老式汽车
hybrid car	混合动力汽车
hydrogen fuel cell	氢燃料电池
lithium-ion battery	锂离子电池
nickel-metal hydride battery pack	镍氢电池组

(续)

Phrases and Technical Terms	
oil crisis	石油危机
plug-in HEV	插电式混合动力汽车
racing car	赛车

1.2 Overview of Alternative Fuel Vehicles
替代燃料汽车概述

1.2

Alternative fuels currently commercially available and closely attended can be listed as follows:
- LPG
- CNG
- Methanol
- Hydrogen
- Fuel-cell
- Electricity Energy
- Hybrid (electricity + conventional fuels)

LPG

Liquefied petroleum gas (LPG) is produced during the normal refining of crude oil. It is 100 percent octane (by comparison, unleaded petrol is 97 percent). LPG is stored under pressure as a liquid, as this is 250 times denser than as a gas so it needs less space to be stored in the car.

Several car manufacturers supply LPG cars direct from the dealership as part of their range. Some other manufacturers without actual LPG vehicles as part of their range will allow conversions to be carried out after manufacture. Cars that run on LPG usually also run on petrol or diesel as well. These types of vehicles are usually referred to as "dual fuel".

CNG

The natural gas contains methane as the major component. Compared to gasoline, compressed natural gas (CNG) is cleaner, less expensive, and generally comes from domestic reserves. So it is considered to be an attractive alternative fuel. However, CNG vehicles require a special refueling infrastructure, and tend to have higher greenhouse gas emissions than hybrids.

Methanol

Methanol can be produced from natural resources like coal and natural gas, and is therefore one of the most attractive candidate fuels. The greatest advantage of the methanol fuel is that it has a liquid phase under normal temperature range, and also it can be available for both spark ignition and compression ignition engines; though its energy density is nearly a half of gasoline or diesel fuel. As a transitional technology before the infrastructure is established for methanol supply, flexible fuel vehicles (FFV) are under development, which can run on M85, gasoline (M0) or any combination in between.

Hydrogen

Hydrogen can be an ideal clean fuel, which emits neither CO_2, nor HC responsible for ozone formation. But today hydrogen is mostly produced from methane and a substantial volume of CO_2 is generated as a by-product. If hydrogen is produced through electrical decomposition of water utilizing solar energy, it can be a truly clean and inexhaustible energy.

The biggest problem with the direct use of hydrogen, as an alternative fuel in a car, is the fuel storage on the vehicle. Another headache with hydrogen is its short travel range; even liquefied hydrogen of the highest energy density would hardly permit one-fourth of the mileage of gasoline vehicle.

Hydrogen is difficult to store and distribute, so it would be much more convenient if fuel cells could use fuels that are more readily available. This problem is addressed by a device called a reformer. A reformer turns hydrocarbon or alcohol fuels into hydrogen, which is then fed to the fuel cell. Unfortunately, reformers are not perfect. They generate heat and produce other gases besides hydrogen.

Fuel-cell

A fuel cell is an electrochemical energy conversion device. A fuel cell converts the chemicals hydrogen and oxygen into water, and in the process it produces electricity. The fuel cell is powered with pure hydrogen, but hydrogen is difficult to store and distribute. Methanol is a liquid fuel that has similar properties to gasoline. It is just as easy to transport and distribute, so methanol may be a likely candidate to power fuel-cell cars.

Electrical Energy

The basic principle of an electric car is that it is powered by an electric motor rather than a petrol or diesel engine. The electric car itself is non-polluting and an attractive transportation means from the standpoint of preserving urban environment. Electric cars run purely on electrical energy generated by large battery units. The electric car has one or sometimes two large AC motors and a single- or double-speed reduction gearbox to drive the wheels.

Hybrid

The energy density of the power battery of an electric car poses serious problems; its travel range per full charge may be more or less 100km. So, a form of transportation called "hybrid" that combines two or more forms of power and converts this into propulsion power in a direct or indirect way is deploying widely. These hybrid vehicles often use internal combustion engine and electric motor or motors to drive the wheels. The majority of today's hybrid cars are petrol-electric, but as technology advances we are seeing diesel-electric hybrid cars.

New Words		
address	[ə'dres]	n. 地址; v. 处理
alcohol	['ælkəhɒl]	n. 乙醇, 酒精
by-product	['baɪprɒdʌkt]	n. 副产品, 意外结果
candidate	['kændɪdət]	n. 候选人
decomposition	[ˌdiːkɒmpə'zɪʃn]	n. 分解
electrochemical	[ɪˌlektrəʊ'kemɪkəl]	adj. 电化学的
headache	['hedeɪk]	n. 头痛; 令人头痛的事
hydrocarbon	[ˌhaɪdrə'kɑːbən]	n. 碳氢化合物, 烃
hydrogen	['haɪdrədʒən]	n. 氢
inexhaustible	[ˌɪnɪg'zɔːstəbl]	adj. 无穷无尽的, 用不完的
infrastructure	['ɪnfrəstrʌktʃə(r)]	n. 基础设施; 基础建设
methane	['miːθeɪn]	n. 甲烷
methanol	['meθənɒl]	n. 甲醇
octane	['ɒkteɪn]	n. 辛烷
power	['paʊə(r)]	n. 功率, 动力, 权力; vt. 运转
propulsion	[prə'pʌlʃn]	n. 推进, 推进力
reformer	[rɪ'fɔːmə(r)]	n. 改革者, 改良者; 重整炉
transportation	[ˌtrænspɔː'teɪʃn]	n. 运送, 运输; 运输工具

Phrases and Technical Terms	
diesel fuel	柴油燃料
from the standpoint of	从……的角度来看
responsible for	导致，是造成……的原因
spark ignition engine	点燃式发动机
power battery	动力电池
be referred to as	叫作，称为
flexible fuel vehicles (FFV)	灵活燃料汽车
energy density	能量密度
fuel-cell car	燃料电池汽车
dual fuel	双燃料（汽车）
solar energy	太阳能
greenhouse gas	温室气体
compression ignition engine	压燃式发动机
compressed natural gas	压缩天然气
liquefied petroleum gas	液化石油气
transportation means	运输工具

1.3 Classifications of Electric Vehicles
电动汽车的分类

1.3

Electric vehicles are broadly categorized into four groups based on the electric design of their powertrains, namely battery electric vehicles (BEVs), plug-in hybrid electric vehicles (PHEVs), hybrid electric vehicles (HEVs), and fuel-cell electric vehicles (FCEVs). Only BEVs and PHEVs are plug-capable, and are referred to as plug-in electric vehicles (PEVs).

1.3.1 Battery Electric Vehicles 纯电动汽车

BEVs also known as pure electric vehicles, full electric vehicles or electric vehicles (EVs), are powered by an electric motor and do not employ an internal combustion engine, as shown in Figure 1.5. The battery provided electric energy to the motor and used as the energy storage unit of a BEV is charged primarily by the power grid and partially via regenerative braking.

Battery electric vehicles do not have tailpipe emissions; therefore, they are also called zero-emission vehicles. In order to facilitate reasonable driving ranges, the BEVs typically have the largest battery packs compared to other models. The size of these battery packs usually varies between 20 kW·h and 85 kW·h with all-electric-range (AER) of 80 – 300 miles.

Currently, a variety of commercial battery electric vehicles are available in the market.

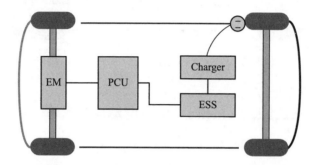

Figure 1.5　Drive train schematic diagram of BEV

1.3.2　Hybrid Electric Vehicles　混合动力汽车

HEVs are primarily powered by internal combustion engines, which use conventional fuels such as gasoline and diesel. These vehicles are also equipped with battery packs, which are charged by regenerative braking systems and are mainly used to enhance the fuel efficiency of the vehicle. The first generation of HEVs was presented to the market in 1997, when Toyota introduced the Prius model, and two years later Honda introduced the Insight model. As of mid-2015 more than 10 million HEVs were deployed worldwide.

1.3.3　Plug-in Hybrid Electric Vehicles　插电式混合动力汽车

As shown in Figure 1.6, PHEVs employ both an electric motor and an internal combustion engine (ICE), which can use gasoline or diesel. Typically, PHEV batteries are smaller than those of BEVs, because the required driving range is mostly supported by internal combustion engines and their combined driving range is higher than that of BEVs. As a result, the main advantage of PHEVs is employing both engines types, which helps the consumers overcome range anxiety. In PHEVs, the electric motor is used mostly in urban environments where driving involves frequent stops. On the other hand, an internal combustion engine is used when the battery is depleted, during intensive cooling or heating, or during rapid acceleration.

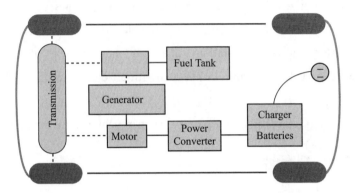

Figure 1.6 Drive train schematic diagram of PHEV

1.3.4 Fuel-Cell Electric Vehicles 燃料电池电动汽车

FCEVs use fuel cells, typically hydrogen, to power their onboard electric motors or charge their storage units as shown in Figure 1.7. The propulsion system in FCEVs is more efficient than those in the conventional ICEVs, and they do not emit any pollutants. FCEVs can be fueled within 10 minutes and they can drive up to 300 miles. Over the last few years, a number of car manufacturers and government agencies have supported research and development activities that accelerate fuel-cell technology. Unlike BEVs and PHEVs, the FCEVs do not use power grid to charge their batteries. Also, their onboard batteries are fairly small in size compared to those of BEVs, PHEVs, and HEVs. The disadvantages of FCEVs include having limited networks of hydrogen fueling stations and the technology being still in its infancy stages.

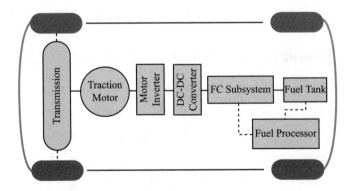

Figure 1.7 Drive train schematic diagram of FCEV

Chapter 1
Overview of the New Energy Vehicles

New Words		
acceleration	[ək,selə'reɪʃn]	n. 加速，加速度
anxiety	[æn'zaɪəti]	n. 焦虑，忧虑
categorize	['kætəgəraɪz]	vt. 分类
charge	[tʃɑːdʒ]	vt. 充电；n. 电荷
charger	['tʃɑːdʒə(r)]	n. 充电器，增压器
converter	[kən'vɜːtə(r)]	n. 变换器，变压器
deplete	[dɪ'pliːt]	vt. &vi. 耗尽，用尽
deploy	[dɪ'plɔɪ]	vt. & vi. 使展开，有效地利用
employ	[ɪm'plɔɪ]	vt. 雇用，使用，利用
facilitate	[fə'sɪlɪteɪt]	vt. 促进，助长，帮助
frequent	['friːkwənt]	adj. 频繁的
fuel	['fjuːəl]	n. 燃料；vt. 给……加燃料；vi. 补充燃料
gasoline	['gæsəliːn]	n. 汽油
grid	[grɪd]	n. 格子，格栅；管网，电网
infancy	['ɪnfənsi]	n. 婴儿期，摇篮时代，初期
intensive	[ɪn'tensɪv]	adj. 强烈的
inverter	[ɪn'vɜːtə]	n. 逆变器，变频器
mostly	['məʊstli]	adv. 大部分，主要地，基本上
onboard	[ˌɒn'bɔːd]	adj. 随车携带的，车载的
pollutant	[pə'luːtənt]	n. 污染物
powertrain	['paʊə(r)treɪn]	n. 动力传动系

Phrases and Technical Terms	
all-electric-range (AER)	全电续驶里程
as of	截止
battery electric vehicle (BEV)	纯电动汽车
battery pack	电池组
DC-DC converter	直流-直流变换器
drive train	传动系统
driving range	续驶里程
energy storage unit	储能装置
fuel efficiency	燃料经济性，燃料效率
fuel-cell electric vehicles (FCEV)	燃料电池电动汽车

(续)

Phrases and Technical Terms	
full electric vehicle	纯电动汽车，全电动汽车
hybrid electric vehicles（HEV）	混合动力汽车
hydrogen fueling station	加氢站
motor inverter	电机逆变器
plug-in electric vehicles（PEV）	插电式电动汽车
plug-in hybrid electric vehicle（PHEV）	插电式混合动力汽车
power grid	电网，电力网
pure electric vehicle	纯电动汽车
regenerative braking	再生制动
schematic diagram	原理图，示意图
traction motor	推进电动机
zero-emission vehicle	零排放汽车

*1 The decline of the electric vehicle was brought about by several major developments, such as a better system of roads in America by the 1920s, lower gasoline car price than electric cars due to the initiation of mass production of internal combustion engine vehicles by Henry Ford, the discovery of Texas crude oil and the invention of the electric starter in 1912 eliminating the need for the hand crank.

【句子分析】句子虽然很长，但结构并不复杂。such as 引出 several major developments 的四个同位语，这四个同位语为名词短语或动名词复合结构。

【参考译文】电动汽车走下坡路是由几个重要的发展所引起的，例如，20 世纪 20 年代的美国道路系统变得更好；亨利·福特开始大规模生产内燃机汽车，从而导致汽油车价格低于电动汽车；得克萨斯州发现了原油，以及 1912 年发明起动机，不再需要手摇起动。

*2 Zero-emission vehicles using an electric powertrain system based on hydrogen fuel cells or purely battery electric systems that are fully competitive to conventional vehicles regarding performance and ease-of-use represent the ultimate target of the future strategy as shown in Figure 1.4.

【句子分析】主语后面有个定语从句 that are fully competitive to conventional vehicles regarding performance and ease-of-use，谓语是 represent。

【参考译文】使用基于氢燃料电池的电动动力系统或纯电池电动系统的零排放车辆在性能和易用性方面可与传统车辆相媲美，它们是未来汽车发展战略的终极目标，如图 1-4 所示。

Chapter 2

Power Batteries of EVs
电动汽车动力电池

2.1 Basic Terminology and Types of Power Batteries
动力电池的基本术语和类型

2.1

2.1.1 Basic Battery Terminology　电池基本术语

There exist certain definitions and measures that quantify and characterize the performance of the batteries for automotive applications.

- Cells, modules, and packs are the central physical components of a PEV battery. A cell is the smallest possible battery that contains electrodes, a separator, and an electrolyte. The output voltage of a typical cell varies from one to six volts. A module consists of multiple cells that are usually connected in either series or parallel. Similarly, a pack is composed of a few modules located in a single location.
- Ampere-hour (A·h) capacity is the amount of charge transferred by one-ampere flow during one hour. Another frequently used capacity term is the rated watt-hour capacity, which is the product of rated Ampere-hour capacity and rated battery voltage. A higher battery capacity provides longer driving ranges, and it also takes more time to charge the battery.
- State of charge (SOC) is an indicator of battery degradation over time, which can be caused due to operating conditions. Accurate gauging is critical for battery management systems. SOC measures the ratio of the present battery capacity with respect to maximum capacity, and is calculated according to

$$SOC = \frac{\text{Present Amount of Charge}}{\text{Total Amount of Usable Charge}}$$

- Depth of discharge (DOD) is used to represent the percentage of discharged capacity. Hence

$$DOD = 1 - SOC$$

Deep-cycle batteries are usually discharged to 80% or higher.
- State of health (SOH) is used to represent the ratio of the maximum charge capacity to its ideal conditions. The SOH indicates the performance degradations of the battery, which is also related to its remaining lifetime.
- Cycle life is the number of charge-discharge cycles that a battery can accommodate within the desired performance regions. Cycle life is determined for a particular DOD, which is typically around 80%. Actual life of the battery can be shorter due to undesired operating conditions such as high temperature and humidity.
- Calendar life is the number of calendar years that a battery is expected to last, and it depends on the SOC and the operating temperature.
- Specific energy represents the amount of energy that can be stored in a unit mass, and it is often measured with the physical dimension watt-hours per kilogram (W·h/kg). It is computed according to

$$\text{Specific Energy} = \frac{\text{Rated A·h Capacity} \times \text{Rated Battery Voltage}}{\text{Battery Mass in kg}}$$

Specific energy, which is also referred to as the gravimetric energy density, is an indicator of the battery chemistry and packaging, which determines the additional weight introduced by the battery for a desired all-electric-range[*1]. It is one of the most important metrics for assessing the PEV performance.
- Specific power is the metric used to define the maximum available power per unit mass, and it is often expressed in watts per kilogram (W/kg). Specific power, sometimes also referred to as gravimetric power density, can be calculated via

$$\text{Specific Power} = \frac{\text{Rated Peak Power}}{\text{Battery Mass in kg}}$$

Specific power determines the battery weight for particular PEV performance measures such as acceleration and regenerative braking.
- Energy density of a battery is the nominal energy per unit volume, and it is represented by watt-hour per liter (W·h/L). Energy density, or volumetric energy density, determines the physical space required to achieve a particular performance target such as driving range.

- power density is the maximum available power per unit volume of the battery, and it is represented by watt per liter (W/L).
- Maximum continuous discharge current is the peak current at which the battery is depleted uninterruptedly. This parameter also serves as a threshold that prevents excessive discharge rates, and therefore, protects the battery life. Moreover, maximum continuous discharge current, along with the specifications of the electric motor, determine the top speed and the acceleration of the PEV.
- Maximum 30-second discharge pulse current is the maximum current at which the battery can be discharged with pulses up to 30 seconds. This limit is determined by the manufacturer to protect the battery's lifetime. Similar to the previous performance measure, it affects the acceleration performance of the vehicle.

2.1.2 Types of Power Batteries 动力电池类型

Possible energy accumulators of BEVs and HEVs are:
- chemical energy accumulator: conventional fuel tank (only for HEVs).
- electrical energy accumulator: battery, high-performance capacitor.
- mechanical energy accumulator: flywheel, hydraulic accumulator.

Electrical energy accumulators are charged during generator operation of an electrical machine. During motor-driven operation, the stored electric energy is fed back to the powertrain.

Among electric energy accumulators, the following technologies are the most competitive:
- lithium-ion batteries (Li-ion).
- nickel-metal hydride batteries (NiMH).
- high-performance double-layer capacitors ("ultracaps" or "supercaps").

Now, there are three types of battery available for use in electric vehicles: lead-acid battery, nickel-based (nickel-cadmium or nickel-metal hydride) battery, and lithium (lithium-ion or lithium-polymer) battery.

Mechanical energy accumulators have so far served primarily to assist moving-off. They are used to accumulate braking energy in vehicles which must start and stop frequently, such as city buses. The mechanical energy of the flywheel or gyro-accumulator is converted into electric energy and feeds the electric motor. Flywheels can pose a security risk in the vehicle however because of their high speeds and resultantly high kinetic energy.

New Words		
accommodate	[əˈkɒmədeɪt]	v. 容纳
accumulate	[əˈkjuːmjəleɪt]	vt. & vi. 堆积，积累
calculate	[ˈkælkjuleɪt]	vt. & vi. 计算，估计
cell	[sel]	n. 电池，单体电池
characterize	[ˈkærəktəraɪz]	vt. 描述……的特性
definition	[ˌdefɪˈnɪʃn]	n. 定义
degradation	[ˌdegrəˈdeɪʃn]	n. 恶化
discharge	[dɪsˈtʃɑːdʒ]	vt. 放电，卸船
electrode	[ɪˈlektrəʊd]	n. 电极
electrolyte	[ɪˈlektrəlaɪt]	n. 电解液，电解质
gauging	[ˈgeɪdʒɪŋ]	n. 测量［试］，测定
gyro-accumulator	[ˌdʒaɪrəʊ-əˈkjuːmjəleɪtə(r)]	n. 陀螺蓄能器
indicator	[ˈɪndɪkeɪtə(r)]	n. 指示器，指标，指示灯
measure	[ˈmeʒə(r)]	n. 度量，度量单位
metric	[ˈmetrɪk]	n. 度量标准，尺度
module	[ˈmɒdjuːl]	n. 模块，模组，组件
moving-off	[ˈmuːvɪŋɒf]	n. 移离，起步
nominal	[ˈnɒmɪnl]	adj. 名义上的，标称的
pack	[pæk]	n. 包裹，一组
packaging	[ˈpækɪdʒɪŋ]	n. 包装
parameter	[pəˈræmɪtə(r)]	n. 参数，参量
quantify	[ˈkwɒntɪfaɪ]	vt. 确定数量，量化
represent	[ˌreprɪˈzent]	vt. 表现，象征；代表
security	[sɪˈkjʊərəti]	n. 安全
separator	[ˈsepəreɪtə(r)]	n. 隔板，分离器
terminology	[ˌtɜːmɪˈnɒlədʒi]	n. 术语
uninterruptedly	[ˌʌnɪntəˈrʌptɪdli]	adv. 不间断地

Phrases and Technical Terms

ampere-hour (A·h) capacity	安·时容量
be composed of	由……组成
calendar life	历年寿命
city bus	城市公共汽车
cycle life	循环寿命
deep-cycle battery	深度循环蓄电池
depth of discharge (DOD)	放电深度
double-layer capacitor	双层电容器
electrical machine	电机
energy accumulator	蓄能器，储能系统
fuel tank	燃料箱
hydraulic accumulator	液压蓄能器
lead-acid battery	铅酸蓄电池
lithium battery	锂电池
lithium-polymer battery	锂聚合物电池
nickel-based battery	镍电池
operating condition	工作条件，工作状况
over time	随着时间的推移
power density	功率密度
specific energy	比能量
specific power	比功率
state of charge (SOC)	荷电状态
state of health (SOH)	健康状态
with respect to	关于，相对于

2.2 Battery Construction and Principle
电池结构与原理

2.2.1 Lead-acid Battery 铅酸蓄电池

The lead-acid battery is widely used as a power battery in industrial trucks and can be used as auxiliary battery on the HEV, to start the IC engine and supply the electrical energy to the load.

Construction

A lead-acid battery consists of positive plates, negative plates, separators, electrolyte and case, see Figure 2.1.

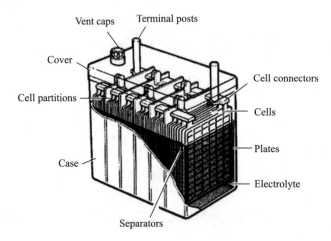

Figure 2.1 Battery construction

Principle

When a lead-acid cell is undergoing charging or discharging, certain chemical changes take place.

These can be indicated by one total chemical reaction equation:

$$\underset{\text{positive plates}}{PbO_2} + \underset{\text{negative plates}}{Pb} + \underset{\text{electrolyte}}{2H_2SO_4} \leftrightarrow \underset{\text{positive plates}}{PbSO_4} + \underset{\text{negative plates}}{PbSO_4} + \underset{\text{electrolyte}}{2H_2O}$$

This two-way or reversible chemical reaction (charged on the left and discharged on the right), describes the full process of the charge and discharge cycle of the lead-acid cell.

2.2.2 Nickel-metal Hydride (NiMH) Battery 镍氢电池

Most battery and hybrid electric vehicles use dual-voltage electrical systems. The high-voltage (HV) system is used to power the electric drive (traction) motor, while a conventional 12-volt system is used to power all other aspects of vehicle operation. One advantage to using this system is that the vehicle can use any conventional electrical accessories in its design.

Most current production HEVs use nickel-metal hydride (NiMH) battery as the high-voltage power battery. NiMH batteries are being used for these applications because of their performance characteristics such as specific energy, cycle life, and safety. From a manufacturing perspective, the NiMH battery is attractive because the materials used in its construction are plentiful and recyclable.

Construction

As shown in Figure 2.2, nickel-metal hydride (NiMH) battery cell uses a positive electrode made of nickel hydroxide and potassium hydroxide electrolyte. The nominal voltage of a NiMH battery cell is 1.2 volts. The negative electrode is unique, however, in that it is a hydrogen-absorbing alloy, also known as a metal hydride.

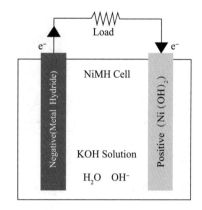

Figure 2.2 A NiMH battery cell

NiMH batteries are known as alkaline batteries due to the alkaline (pH greater than 7) nature of the electrolyte. The electrolyte is aqueous potassium hydroxide. Potassium hydroxide works very well for this application because it does not corrode the other parts of the battery and can be housed in a sealed steel container. Also, potassium hydroxide does not take part in the chemical reaction of the battery, so the electrolyte concentration stays constant at any given state of charge.

There are two primary designs of a NiMH battery cell. These are:

(1) Cylindrical type (Figure 2.3) The cylindrical type has the active materials made in long ribbons and arranged in a spiral fashion inside a steel cylinder (case). The negative electrode is wound alongside the positive electrode, and the separator material holding the electrolyte is placed between them. The negative electrode is attached to the steel battery case, while the positive electrode is attached to the (−) terminal at the top of the battery. There is a self-resealing safety vent located at the top of the battery case, which will relieve internal pressure in case of overcharge, short circuiting, reverse charge, or other abuse. Cylindrical cells are most often incorporated into modules with a group of six cells connected in series. This creates a single battery module with a 7.2-volt output. Groups of these modules can then be connected in series to create higher voltage battery packs.

(2) Prismatic type (Figure 2.4) The prismatic type is a rectangular or boxlike design with the active materials formed into flat plates, much like a conventional lead-acid battery. The positive and negative plates are placed alternately in the battery case, with tabs used to connect the plate groups. Separator material is placed between the plates to prevent them from touching but still allow electrolyte to circulate freely.

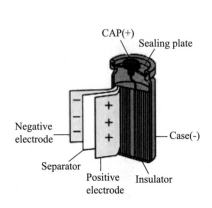
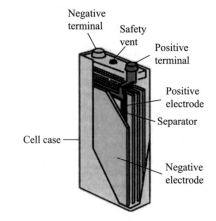

Figure 2.3　NiMH battery cell-cylindrical type　　　Figure 2.4　NiMH battery cell-prismatic type

Principle

Operation of a NiMH battery cell is shown in Figure 2.5.

During battery charging, hydrogen ions (protons) travel from the positive electrode to the negative electrode, where they are absorbed into the metal hydride material. The electrolyte does not participate in the reaction and acts only as a medium for the hydrogen ions to travel through.

During battery discharging, this process reverses, with the hydrogen ions (protons) traveling from the negative electrode back to the positive electrode. The density of the electrodes changes somewhat during the charge-discharge process, but this is kept to a minimum as only protons are exchanged during battery cycling. Electrode stability due to minimal density changes is one of the reasons why the NiMH battery has very good cycle life.

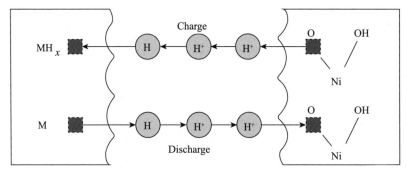

Figure 2.5　Chemical reactions inside a NiMH cell

2.2.3 Lithium-ion (Li-ion) Battery 锂离子蓄电池

The lithium-ion (Li-ion) battery technology shows a great deal of promise for electric vehicles (EV) and hybrid electric vehicles (HEV) applications. Lithium-ion batteries have approximately twice the specific energy of nickel-metal hydride, good high temperature performance, and high nominal cell voltage (3.6V or three times that of nickel-based alkaline batteries).

Construction

The basic component of a Li-ion battery is a cell, as shown in Figure 2.6, and each cell has five basic components that facilitate the energy conversion process. The first component is an anode, which gives up the electrons to an external circuit (e.g., electric motor) and oxidizes during the reaction. The second component is a cathode, which accepts the electrons from the external circuit. The third component is the electrolyte which completes ion transfer inside the cells. The fourth component is a membrane that acts a separator and prevents the internal short circuits between the anode and the cathode, and the last component is a container, which is devised for safety purposes.

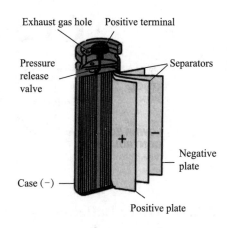

Figure 2.6 A Li-ion battery cell

In a typical battery, the positive electrode is made up of lithium and transition metal material.

The original Li-ion cell design used lithium cobalt oxide for its cathode, which has good energy storage characteristics but suffers chemical breakdown at relatively low temperatures. One of the more promising cathode designs for automotive applications is lithium iron phosphate ($LiFePO_4$), which is stable at higher temperatures and releases less energy when it does suffer breakdown. Currently, lithium nickel cobalt manganate ($LiNiCoMnO_2$) is widely used as a cathode material. Graphite is widely employed as the negative electrode material.

Principle

In Li-ion batteries, electrical energy is generated through electrochemical oxidation-reduction reactions. During the charging stage, lithium ions move from the positive electrode, pass through the electrolyte, and intercalate between graphite layers, and enter the negative electrode. During the discharge process, the reverse process takes place (Figure 2.7), and the stored energy is used to run the electric motor.

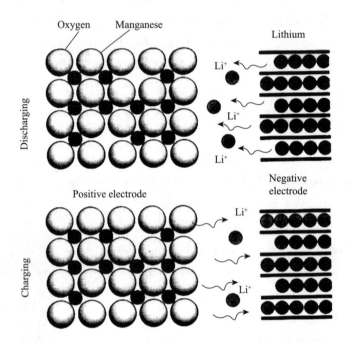

Figure 2.7 Chemical reaction process of a Li-ion battery

2.2.4 Other Batteries 其他蓄电池

High voltage batteries which can be used to power battery electric vehicles and hybrid electric vehicles also include nickel-cadmium (Ni-Cd) battery, lithium-polymer (Li-poly) battery, Zinc-air battery and ZEBRA battery (a sodium-metal-chloride battery).

A comparison of specific energy and nominal voltage for the various battery technologies can be seen in the Table 2.1.

Table 2.1 A comparison for the various battery technologies

Battery type	Nominal voltage per cell/V	Theoretical specific energy/ (W·h/kg)	Practical specific energy/ (W·h/kg)	Major issues
Lead-acid	2.1	252	35	Heavy, low cycle life, toxic materials
Nickel-metal hydride	1.2	278 – 800	80	Cost, high self-discharge rate, memory effect

(续)

Battery type	Nominal voltage per cell/V	Theoretical specific energy/ (W·h/kg)	Practical specific energy/ (W·h/kg)	Major issues
Lithium-ion	3.6	766	120	Safety issues, calendar life, cost
Nickel-cadmium	1.2	244	50	Toxic materials, cost
Zinc-air	1.1	1320	110	Low power, limited cycle life, bulky
Sodium-sulfur	2.0	792	100	High-temperature battery, safety, low power electrolyte
Sodium-metal-chloride (ZEBRA)	2.5	787	90	High temperature operation, low power

New Words

abuse	[ə'bju:s]	n. 滥用
accessory	[ək'sesəri]	n. 附件
alongside	[ə,lɒŋ'saɪd]	adv. 与……并排; prep. 在……旁边
anode	['ænəʊd]	n. 阳极
aqueous	['eɪkwɪəs]	adj. 水的, 水成的
auxiliary	[ɔ:g'zɪliəri]	adj. 辅助的
cathode	['kæθəʊd]	n. 阴极
concentration	[,kɒnsn'treɪʃn]	n. 浓度
corrode	[kə'rəʊd]	vt. & vi. 腐蚀, 侵蚀
cylindrical	[sə'lɪndrɪkl]	adj. 圆柱形的
describe	[dɪs'kraɪb]	v. 描写, 叙述
equation	[ɪ'kweɪʒn]	n. 方程式, 等式
graphite	['græfaɪt]	n. 石墨
membrane	['membreɪn]	n. 薄膜, 隔膜
participate	[pɑ:'tɪsɪpeɪt]	vi. 参加
perspective	[pə'spektɪv]	n. 观点, 看法
plentiful	['plentɪfl]	adj. 丰富的; 富产的
prismatic	[prɪz'mætɪk]	adj. 棱镜的; 棱形

(续)

New Words		
promise	['prɒmɪs]	n. 许诺；希望
proton	['prəʊtɒn]	n. 质子
recyclable	[ˌriː'saɪkləbl]	adj. 可循环再用的
ribbon	['rɪbən]	n. 带
spiral	['spaɪrəl]	n. 螺旋（线）；adj. 螺旋形的
tab	[tæb]	n. 凸舌，连接片
undergo	[ˌʌndə'gəʊ]	v. 经历，承受

Phrases and Technical Terms	
alkaline battery	碱性电池
auxiliary battery	辅助蓄电池
chemical reaction equation	化学反应方程
IC engine	内燃机
in case of	万一，如果
industrial truck	工业车辆
lithium cobalt oxide	钴酸锂（$LiCoO_2$）
lithium iron phosphate	磷酸铁锂（$LiFePO_4$）
lithium nickel cobalt manganate	三元锂（镍钴锰酸锂）（$LiNiCoMnO_2$）
metal hydride	金属氢化物
negative electrode	负极
nickel-cadmium (Ni-Cd) battery	镍镉（Ni-Cd）电池
nickel-metal hydride (NiMH) battery	镍氢（NiMH）电池，金属氢化物镍蓄电池
oxidation-reduction reaction	氧化还原反应
participate in	参加
positive electrode	正极
steel cylinder	钢筒，钢瓶
take part in	参加，参与

Chapter 2
Power Batteries of EVs

2.3 Battery Management and Cooling Systems
电池管理与冷却系统

2.3.1 Battery Management Systems (BMS) 电池管理系统

The BMS should monitor, control, and communicate with the battery. Therefore, the primary functions of a BMS are:

- Under-voltage and over-voltage protections.
- Short circuit protection.
- Thermal protection.
- Cell balancing.
- Controlling battery charging and discharging.
- Determining battery SOC and SOH.
- Safety protection.

Figure 2.8 demonstrates a block diagram of a generic BMS. In order to perform the functions listed, the sensing unit gathers some information such as voltage and temperature from the battery, and communicates them to the management and the balancing units. The role of the balancing unit is to ensure that cell voltages operate within the allowed limits. Voltage, current, and temperature readings are used to determine the SOC levels of the batteries.

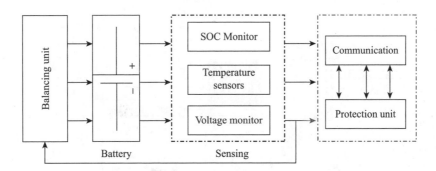

Figure 2.8 A block diagram of a generic BMS

Cell balancing is an important part of battery management systems. In a typical PEV battery, several cells are connected in parallel and act as a block to meet the high capacity requirements, while several cells are wired in series to meet high voltage requirements. Moreover, each cell can have different properties due to chemical offsets. Therefore, cells may have different voltage levels, which may degrade batteries' lifetimes or even cause life-threatening incidents. Cell balancing is required to balance cell voltages, and subsequently, prevent such unwanted consequences.

In a battery system developed by Nissan and Sony engineers, as shown in Figure 2.9, cell controllers and battery controller work together to calculate battery power and remaining capacity, and convey the results to the vehicle control unit, charging current bypass circuit are also controlled on cell-to-cell basis.

Toyota hybrid car battery management system is shown in Figure 2.10.

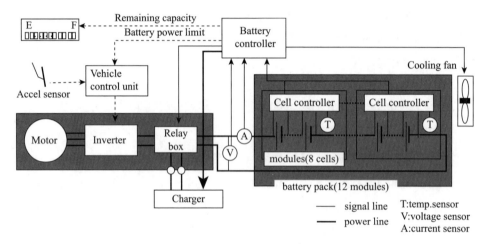

Figure 2.9 A battery management system

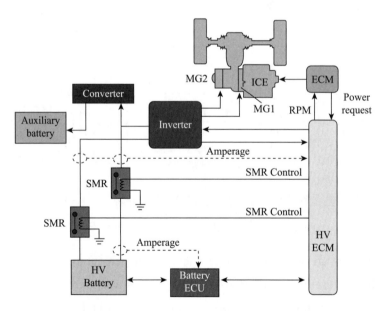

Figure 2.10 Toyota hybrid car battery management system

2.3.2 Battery Cooling Systems 电池冷却系统

High operating temperatures of HV NiMH battery can lower performance and cause damage to a NiMH battery pack. All current production HEVs use air cooling to control HV battery pack temperature. Cabin air is circulated over the battery cells using an electric fan and ducting inside the vehicle, as shown in Figure 2.11.

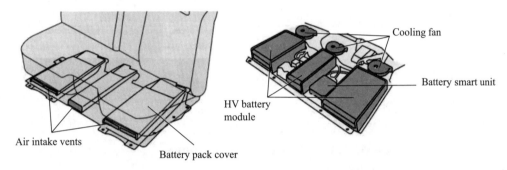

Figure 2.11 Battery cooling system for a Toyota hybrid SUV

Temperature sensors are mounted in various locations in the battery pack housing to send data to the module responsible for controlling battery temperature. These inputs are used to help determine battery charge rate and cooling fan operation.

New Words		
communicate	[kəˈmjuːnɪkeɪt]	vi. 通信,相连,互通
convey	[kənˈveɪ]	vt. 传达,传送
gather	[ˈgæðə(r)]	vt. 收集
life-threatening	[laɪf ˈθretnɪŋ]	adj. 威胁生命的
offset	[ˈɒfset]	n. 偏移,偏离,偏差

Phrases and Technical Terms	
balancing unit	平衡装置
battery controller	蓄电池控制器
battery management system (BMS)	电池管理系统 (BMS)
block diagram	框图
cabin air	车内空气

Phrases and Technical Terms	
cell controller	单体电池控制器
HV battery pack	高压电池组
remaining capacity	剩余容量
sensing unit	传感装置
temperature sensor	温度传感器

2.4 Battery Charging Technology
电池充电技术

2.4

2.4.1 Categories of Battery Charging Technology
电池充电技术的分类

Battery charging technologies can be categorized, broadly, into onboard and off-board charging. Both charging technologies can be further divided into two groups, where one allows only unidirectional power flow, and the other one enables bidirectional power flow.

Onboard chargers are physically located in the PEV. Onboard chargers are used primarily for low charging power levels, which are typically less than 10 kW. Therefore, they do not cause battery heating and, consequently, they protect batteries' health.

On the other hand, off-board chargers are designed for higher charging rates (i.e., 10 – 80 kW) and therefore require more elaborate power electronics architectures. In order to facilitate high levels of charging power, additional infrastructure, such as energy storage units or three-phase lines, might become necessary. The major setback of off-board chargers is that they degrade battery lifetime more quickly than the onboard ones.

Both onboard and off-board chargers can provide unidirectional or bidirectional power flows. Typically, unidirectional chargers have simpler hardware architecture and only allow the grid to charge the battery. Usually, unidirectional chargers employ a diode bridge, a filter, and DC-DC converters. A generic layout of these chargers is presented in Figure 2.12. Bidirectional chargers, in contrast, enable the vehicle to inject power back to the grid, which allows the PEVs to act as mobile storage units.

Chapter 2
Power Batteries of EVs

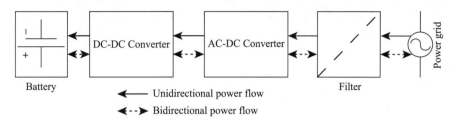

Figure 2.12 Generic layout of the chargers

2.4.2 Wireless Charging Technology 无线充电技术

Wireless charging is an emerging technology and enables PEVs to charge their batteries in a contactless manner. Wireless charging has recently gained some attention mainly because it can allow power transfer between the grid and a vehicle while the vehicle is on the move. During charging, high-frequency magnetic fields between transmitting and receiving coils is required. Typically, the transmitting coils are built into a parking space and the receiving coils are attached to the underbody of the PEVs.

Based on this charging technology, all electric range can be extended without requiring the vehicle to spend time for the charging service and the required battery size can be reduced. Other benefits of wireless charging are that it requires limited interaction with PEV owners and eliminates the hazards associated with cords and electric sparks.

Nevertheless, for wireless charging, the most significant concern is safety. Flux leakage between the transmitting and receiving coils might have health risks for an individual near the coils. Moreover, the efficiency of wireless chargers is lower than the wired chargers and the charging rates are typically slower than the wired ones.

New Words		
architecture	[ˈɑːkɪtektʃə(r)]	n. 结构
bidirectional	[ˌbaɪdəˈrekʃənl]	adj. 双向的
degrade	[dɪˈɡreɪd]	vt. 降低
elaborate	[ɪˈlæbərət]	adj. 复杂的，精心制作的
emerging	[iˈmɜːdʒɪŋ]	adj. 新兴的
underbody	[ˈʌndəˌbɒdɪ]	n. 底部
unidirectional	[ˌjuːnɪdɪˈrekʃənəl]	adj. 单向的

Phrases and Technical Terms	
charging rate	充电率，充电速度
diode bridge	二极管电桥
flux leakage	漏磁
off-board charging	离车充电
onboard charging	车载充电，随车充电
parking space	停车位
power electronics	功率电子器件，控制器
power flow	能流
receiving coil	接收线圈
transmitting coil	发射线圈
wireless charging	无线充电

2.5 Service and Testing
维护与测试

2.5

2.5.1 Safety Precautions 安全措施

Always keep in mind that the high-voltage batteries for an HEV can produce sufficient voltage and current to severely injure or kill.

- Always wear appropriate personal protective equipment (PPE) and use approved safety procedures when working around these batteries.
- Read all warning labels and always follow the vehicle manufacturer's instructions.
- Always refer to the service manual for approved safety procedures when handling the HV battery pack.
- Do not work on the vehicle if moisture is present on the skin or anywhere on or near the vehicle.
- If service must be performed on the high-voltage system, be sure to disconnect the HV battery and allow enough time for system capacitors to discharge before proceeding.
- The battery case contains liquid potassium hydroxide, a strong alkali solution. Any liquid around the battery should be checked with litmus paper to determine if it is an electrolyte spill. If an electrolyte spill has occurred, be sure to disable the HV system, and then use a mixture of vinegar and water to neutralize the solution before

Chapter 2
Power Batteries of EVs

cleaning up with soap and water.
- If an electrical fire occurs, do not attempt to extinguish it using water. Use an ABC fire extinguisher or wait for fire fighters to deal with it.
- Remove any clothing that has come into contact with electrolyte and flush any exposed skin with large amounts of water. If electrolyte comes in contact with the eyes, flush with large amounts of water, but do not use a neutralizing solution. Be sure to seek medical advice to prevent further injury from electrolyte contact.

2.5.2 Battery Pack Service 电池组维护

Preparation before service

Perform the following steps before starting HV battery pack service:
- Remove the safety disconnect switch.
- Wait 15 minutes for capacitors to discharge.
- Wear class zero gloves.

Disassembling battery pack

Adhere the following steps to do this during disassembling battery pack.

Step 1: To depower the high-voltage system, the ignition was off and the negative battery cable was disconnected from the 12-volt auxiliary battery, then the HV battery safety plug was removed.

Step 2: After checking that the voltage level is safe, the rear seat and HV battery cover were removed.

Step 3: Remove the high-voltage wires from the battery pack while wearing HV gloves (Figure 2.13).

Step 4: Remove the HV battery pack through the rear of the vehicle.

Step 5: Place the HV battery pack on a workbench that is covered with a thick rubber (insulating) mat. A wood top bench can also be used.

Step 6: Perform a visual inspection, to be sure that electrical connections between battery modules are corroded, as shown in Figure 2.14.

Figure 2.13 HV gloves

Figure 2.14 Connections between battery modules are corroded

Step 7: Remove the HV battery pack temperature sensors, and remove the HV battery vent tubes from the battery pack.

Step 8: Remove the end caps from the battery pack.

Step 9: Remove the fasteners that hold the battery modules to the base of the battery pack.

Step 10: Remove the end module from the battery pack.

Servicing battery pack

After disassembling the HV battery pack, service work will involve individual battery modules.

- Check the voltage of each module. The individual modules were measured using a voltmeter (Figure 2.15) and most modules were found to be about 3.6 V which is far below the minimum of 5.4 V that most experts think can be restored by charging.
- Do not use battery modules that are below 5.4 volts (10.8 V for a block) which is the lower limit on cell voltage.
- If batteries are below 7.5 volts, charge at a maximum of 16 volts at 2 to 6 ampere rate.
- Monitor battery temperature and do not allow the battery to overheat and do not allow the temperature to exceed 120 °F (50 °C).
- Allow the voltage to stabilize after being charged. Then record the no load voltage to be used for the internal resistance calculation. In this example, assume a voltage of 15.21 volts.
- Use a high wattage resistor to apply a load to the batteries. A 1.5 ohm resistor rated at 25 watts is often used to provide a load.
- Apply the load resistor and measure the new voltage and current values.

Figure 2.15 Individual modules were measured using a voltmeter

Determine the internal resistance

To determine the internal resistance of a battery block (two modules), compare the unloaded voltage to the voltage of the block under the load that was applied by the resistor, which is called the delta (Δ) or the change in the voltage[*2]. This difference is then divided by the measured current (amperes) that was measured during the load test using the 1.5 ohm resistor[*3].

Chapter 2
Power Batteries of EVs

For example, if the current is 9.6 amps with voltage at 15.50 volts, then the internal resistance is:

$$(15.50 - 15.21)V \div 9.6A = 0.0302\Omega = 30.2m\Omega$$

This tested salvage battery can be used to replace a defective battery module in a vehicle that has battery block resistance of 25 to 35 milliohms. Always try to match the internal resistance as close as possible.

Charge a HV battery pack

When a HV battery pack needs to be recharged off vehicle, a special HV battery charger must be used. Before connecting the charger, wear insulated gloves and remove the service plug. Keep the ignition key in your pocket for safety. Connect the charger to the HV battery pack as shown in Figure 2.16.

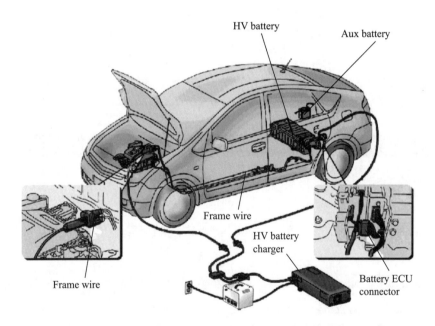

Figure 2.16 2004 & later Prius HV battery charger connection points

New Words		
adhere	[əd'hɪə(r)]	vt. 遵循，坚持
alkali	['ælkəlaɪ]	n. 碱
appropriate	[ə'prəʊpriət]	adj. 适当的，合适的

defective	[dɪˈfektɪv]	adj. 有缺陷的，有瑕疵的
depower		vt. 断电
disable	[dɪsˈeɪbl]	vt. 使无能力
extinguish	[ɪkˈstɪŋgwɪʃ]	vt. 熄灭（火）
fastener	[ˈfɑːsnə(r)]	n. 紧固件
litmus	[ˈlɪtməs]	n. 石蕊
neutralize	[ˈnjuːtrəlaɪz]	vt. 中和
proceed	[prəˈsiːd]	vi. 进行
salvage	[ˈsælvɪdʒ]	n. 经加工后重新利用的废物
spill	[spɪl]	n. 溢出（物，量）
stabilize	[ˈsteɪbəlaɪz]	vt. （使）稳定
unloaded	[ʌnˈləʊdɪd]	adj. 空载的
vinegar	[ˈvɪnɪgə(r)]	n. 醋
voltmeter	[ˈvəʊltmiːtə(r)]	n. 电压表
workbench	[ˈwɜːkbentʃ]	n. 工作台

Phrases and Technical Terms

battery block	电池块，电池子模块
come in [into] to contact with	接触到
fire extinguisher	灭火器
fire fighter	消防员
litmus paper	石蕊试纸
personal protective equipment (PPE)	人身保护设备
potassium hydroxide	氢氧化钾
safety plug	安全插头
service manual	维修手册
service plug	维修插头
warning label	警告标贴

Chapter 2
Power Batteries of EVs

NOTES

*1 Specific energy, which is also referred to as the gravimetric energy density, is an indicator of the battery chemistry and packaging, which determines the additional weight introduced by the battery for a desired all-electric-range.

【句子分析】句中有两个 which… 定语从句，第一个是主语的定语从句，第二个是 indicator 的定语从句。

【参考译文】比能量也被称为重量能量密度，它是衡量电池化学和封装的一个指标，这个指标决定着为获得期望的全电续驶里程由电池所带来的额外重量。

*2 To determine the internal resistance of a battery block (two modules), compare the unloaded voltage to the voltage of the block under the load that was applied by the resistor, which is called the delta (Δ) or the change in the voltage.

【句子分析】首先要注意固定搭配 compare… to…（将……与……进行比较）。其次要注意 that was applied… 和 which is called…这两个定语从句，第一个定语从句的先行词是 load，第二个定语从句的 which 指代它前面的 compare… to… the resistor 即比较的结果或差值。

【参考译文】为确定电池块（两个模块）的内阻，将电池块的空载电压与通过电阻器加负载后（测得）的电压进行比较，得到电压增量（Δ），即电压的变化量。

*3 This difference is then divided by the measured current (amperes) that was measured during the load test using the 1.5 ohm resistor.

【句子分析】句中的 that… 是一个定语从句，that 的先行词是 current。

【参考译文】然后将这个差值除以用 1.5Ω 电阻在负载试验中测得的电流（A）。

Chapter 3

Traction Motors and Controllers
牵引电机与控制器

3.1 Types of Traction Motors
牵引电机的类型

Two types of electric motor are commonly used in electric vehicles: the direct current (DC) motor and the alternating current (AC) motor.

DC motors

In most electric industrial trucks, the series-wound DC motors, as shown in Figure 3.1a, are used. In these motors, the field and armature windings are in series. Representative torque-power-speed characteristics of this type of motor are shown in Figure 3.1b. While the efficiency of the series-wound DC motor is relatively low, it is still being used because of its simple design and low cost.

Separately excited (shunt) DC motors are also used in some electric vehicles.

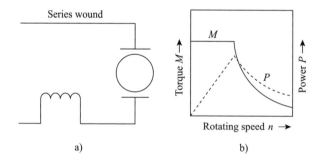

Figure 3.1 The series-wound DC motor and its torque-power-speed characteristics

AC motors

Synchronous or asynchronous AC motors are now the norm as traction motors for passenger vehicles. To convert DC supplied by the battery to AC, an inverter is required. The maintenance cost of these AC motors is lower than that of DC motors, as they do not require brush/commutation or slip-ring system. The synchronous motor with high density, rare-earth permanent magnets mounted on the rotor is widely used in electric or hybrid passenger vehicles. The permanent magnets may be mounted on the surface of the rotor, as shown in Figure 3.2a, or mounted in the interior of the rotor. Interior-mounted permanent magnets are more secure than surface-mounted permanent magnets for high-speed operations.

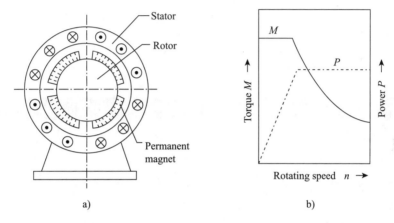

Figure 3.2 The permanent magnet synchronous AC motor and its torque-power-speed characteristics

The permanent magnet synchronous AC motor generally has higher efficiency than the conventional synchronous motor, due to the elimination of the excitation current drawn from the energy source and to the elimination of the ohmic loss in the rotor winding (field winding). While rare-earth magnets make the motor more expensive, their use allows compact design with high torques. Representative torque-power-speed characteristics of this type of motor are shown in Figure 3.2b. Characteristics of the permanent magnet synchronous AC motor approach those of the ideal power plant for application to motor vehicles. This also allows the use of a single-stage reduction gear in the drive train.

New Words		
approach	[ə'prəʊtʃ]	vt. & vi. 接近
armature	['ɑːmətʃə(r)]	n. 电枢;转子
asynchronous	[eɪ'sɪŋkrənəs]	adj. 异步的
commutation	[ˌkɒmjuː'teɪʃn]	n. 换向

(续)

New Words		
excitation	[ˌeksaɪˈteɪʃən]	n. 励磁
interior-mounted		adj. 内部安装的，内装式
magnet	[ˈmæɡnət]	n. 磁铁，磁体
rare-earth	[ˈreərˈɜːθ]	n. 稀土
rotor	[ˈrəʊtə(r)]	n. 转子
secure	[sɪˈkjʊə(r)]	adj. 安全的；牢固的
slip-ring		n. 集电环
surface-mounted		adj. 安装在表面上的
synchronous	[ˈsɪŋkrənəs]	adj. 同步的

Phrases and Technical Terms	
armature winding	电枢绕组
asynchronous AC motor	交流异步电机
excitation current	励磁电流
field winding	磁场绕组
motor vehicle	汽车，机动车
ohmic loss	电阻损耗
passenger vehicle	乘用车，载客车辆
permanent magnet	永久磁铁
power plant	发电厂，动力装置
series-wound DC motor	串励直流电机
synchronous AC motor	交流同步电机

3.2 Construction and Principle
结构与原理

3.2

3.2.1 Electric Motor Operation 电机的运行

Basic principle

A current-carrying conductor is placed in a magnetic field, then, it is compelled to move from strong field to weak field. The direction of movement is perpendicular to both the conductor and the magnetic field, see Figure 3.3a. When the conductor formed a loop is placed in a magnetic field, it is compelled to rotate, see Figure 3.3b.

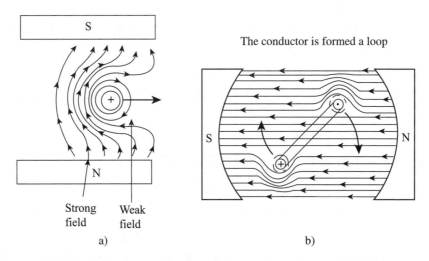

Figure 3.3 A current-carrying conductor placed in a magnetic field

Construction

A simple electric motor is shown in Figure 3.4. The conductive loop that rotates in an electric motor is called an armature. The armature is connected to a ring that is similar to alternator rotor slip rings. However, the slip ring in this simple motor is split into two. This two-piece slip ring causes current to flow through one-half of the split ring, through the loop of wire, to the other half of the split ring. This split slip ring in a motor is referred to as a commutator. Each piece of the commutator is called a commutator segment. Spring-loaded brushes make electrical contact with the commutator segments. The brushes and commutator segments permit the armature to rotate yet still make electrical contact.

The two magnets shown surrounding the armature in Figure 3.4 are electromagnets called pole shoes. Loops of copper conductor called the field coils or field windings are wrapped around the pole shoes. The field coil is wrapped in such a direction to cause the half of the pole shoe facing the armature to become a north pole magnet. The pole shoe on the left side of this illustration has the field coils wrapped such that the side of the pole shoe facing the armature

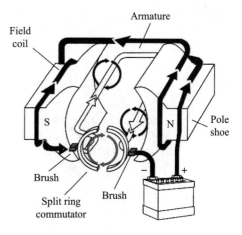

Figure 3.4 A simple motor

becomes a south pole magnet.

Current flows in accordance with such a path:

Positive battery terminal → right side field coil → left side field coil → left side brush → split ring commutator → armature loop → other side of the split ring commutator → right side brush → battery-negative terminal.

The armature, commutator and shaft to which the armature and commutator are installed and rotated together are called rotor. The field coils, pole shoes and brushes are called stator.

3.2.2　AC Asynchronous Motor　交流异步电机

The motor uses electromagnetic induction from the stator to induce a current and therefore creates a magnetic field in the rotor without the need for brushes. An AC asynchronous motor is also known as an AC induction motor (ACIM), because it allows a certain amount of slip between the rotor and the changing magnetic field in the stator. The term asynchronous means that the speed of the motor is not necessarily related to the frequency of the current flowing through the stator windings.

ACIMs include squirrel-cage and wound-rotor induction designs. A squirrel-cage rotor, as shown in Figure 3.5, is composed of parallel thick copper or aluminum conductors connected to a ring of the same material at the ends. As the stator magnetic field rotates, the stator field interacts with the magnetic field of the rotor, causing the rotor to turn at nearly the speed of the rotating stator magnetic field. An alternate design is called the wound rotor, as shown in Figure 3.6. In this case, the rotor has the same number of poles as the stator, and the windings are made of wire. When the stator magnetic field rotates and the rotor windings are shorted, the stator magnetic field motion induces a field in the wound rotor, causing the rotor to turn at nearly the speed of the rotating stator magnetic field.

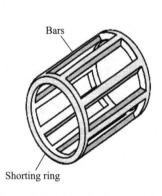

Figure 3.5　A squirrel-cage rotor

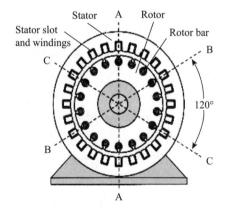

Figure 3.6　A typical motor design with a wound rotor

3.2.3 AC Synchronous Motor 交流同步电机

The AC synchronous motor rotates exactly at the supply frequency or a submultiple of the supply frequency. The speed is controlled by varying the frequency of the AC supply and the number of poles in the stator winding.

An electronic switching circuit produces commutating currents in the stator windings based on the position of the magnetic poles on the rotor. The rotor of the motor rotates at the same speed as the stator commutation. The speed of the motor is controlled by the frequency of the AC current being used.

The brushless permanent magnet synchronous motors produce high starting torque and are typically over 90% efficient. There are two types of rotor designs:

- The permanent magnets are mounted on the outside surface of the rotor, as shown in Figure 3.2a. These are called surface permanent magnets (SPMs).
- The permanent magnets are housed inside the outer shell of the rotor and are called interior permanent magnets (IPMs), The Honda, Ford and Toyota hybrids use an IPM-type rotor assembly.

In both types of motors, the stator coils are stationary and the permanent magnet assembly rotates. Alternating current (AC) is fed to the various phases in the stator in order to get the permanent magnets in the rotor to "chase" the changing magnetic field, as shown in Figure 3.7.

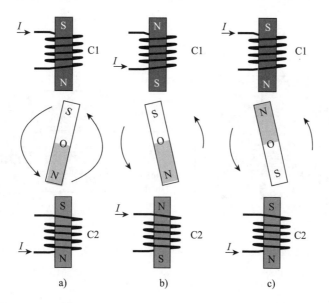

Figure 3.7 The rotor is forced to rotate by changing the polarity and the frequency of the coils surrounding the rotor

The current is fed into one of the three stator phases and flows out of a second phase. This current flows through the phases, acts as a position sensor, and helps the controller to determine when to energize which phase of the stator.

3.2.4 Permanent Magnet Brushless DC Motor
永磁无刷直流电机

In permanent magnet brushless DC motors, the activation and deactivation of the individual windings is carried out with the help of control electronics (electronic switch), see Figure 3.8. The control electronics receive information on the position of the rotor from the rotor position sensor, e.g. a Hall-effect sensor, and activate or deactivate the corresponding windings in the stator, to produce rotating magnetic fields. The speed of the motor depends on the commutation frequency of the commutation device. Electronically commutated DC motors usually have three or more windings.

Advantages of permanent magnet brushless DC motors compared with mechanically commutated motors:

- Possibility of higher rotational speeds.
- Quiet operation, good electromagnetic compatibility and reduced maintenance.
- Diagnostic capability of the control electronics and smooth mechanical running.
- Compact construction and low weight.

Construction of permanent magnet brushless DC motor is shown in Figure 3.9.

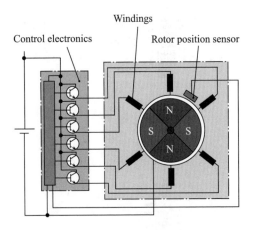

Figure 3.8 Permanent magnet brushless DC motor

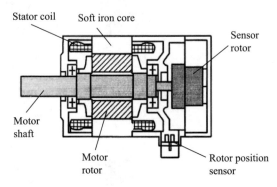

Figure 3.9 Construction of permanent magnet brushless DC motor

New Words

activation	[ˌæktɪˈveɪʃn]	n. 活化，激活
brush	[brʌʃ]	n. 刷子，电刷
brushless	[bˈrʌʃlɪs]	adj. 无刷的
chase	[tʃeɪs]	vi. 追逐，追赶
commutator	[ˈkɒmjuteɪtə(r)]	n. 换向器
compel	[kəmˈpel]	vt. 强迫，迫使
deactivation	[diːæktɪˈveɪʃən]	n. 失活，钝化
electromagnet	[ɪˈlektrəʊmæɡnət]	n. 电磁体，电磁铁
energize	[ˈenədʒaɪz]	vt. 给……加电压，通电
illustration	[ˌɪləˈstreɪʃn]	n. 说明，插图
loop	[luːp]	n. 圈，环，回路
magnetic	[mæɡˈnetɪk]	adj. 有磁性的，磁性的
perpendicular	[ˌpɜːpənˈdɪkjələ(r)]	adj. 垂直的，成直角的
spring-loaded		adj. 受弹簧力作用的
squirrel-cage	[skˈwɪrəlkˈeɪdʒ]	n. 鼠笼式
stator	[ˈsteɪtə]	n. 定子
submultiple	[sʌbˈmʌltɪpl]	n. 约数，因数
wrap	[ræp]	vt. 包；缠绕

Phrases and Technical Terms

AC induction motor (ACIM)	交流感应电机
be perpendicular to	垂直于……
commutator segment	换向器片
current-carrying conductor	载流导体
electromagnetic induction	电磁感应
electronic switch	电子开关
field coil	励磁绕组，磁场绕组
Hall-effect sensor	霍尔效应传感器
interior permanent magnet (IPM)	内部永磁
magnetic field	磁场

Phrases and Technical Terms	
make electrical contact with	与……电接触
permanent magnet brushless DC motor	永磁无刷直流电机
pole shoes	极靴
squirrel-cage rotor	鼠笼式转子
starting torque	起动转矩
surface permanent magnet (SPM)	表面永磁
wound rotor	绕线式转子

3.3 Motor Control System (controllers)
电机控制系统

3.3

3.3.1 Permanent Magnet Brushless DC Motor Controller
永磁无刷直流电机控制器

As shown in Figure 3.10, traction motor controller on Honda hybrid electric vehicles is a motor control module (MCM), which is typical of the controller used in most hybrid electric vehicles. The MCM has three inputs from three rotor position sensors, A, B, and C. They send digital information to the MCM to indicate rotor angular position. The MCM is programmed to use this information to determine which driver circuits in the power drive unit (PDU) (electronic switch) be turned on. The PDU controls all functions of the motor, whether it is producing torque to drive the vehicle or is being used as a generator to charge the batteries during regenerative braking.

The current flow through the PDU is controlled by six insulated gate bipolar transistors (IGBTs). Three of these transistors control the voltage side of the circuit and are called positive or high-side IGBTs. The other three transistors are negative or low-side IGBTs because they are on the negative (ground) side of the stator coils. The base of each IGBT connects to an input terminal in the connector to the PDU. The IGBTs are current drivers that send current from the battery pack through the stator windings to energize the stator coils and move the rotor to power the drive wheels.[*1]

Each IGBT has a diode connected in parallel between the collector and the emitter, as shown in Figure 3.10. These six diodes work together to rectify stator AC to pulsating DC to charge the high-voltage batteries when the DC electric drive motor becomes a generator during regenerative braking.

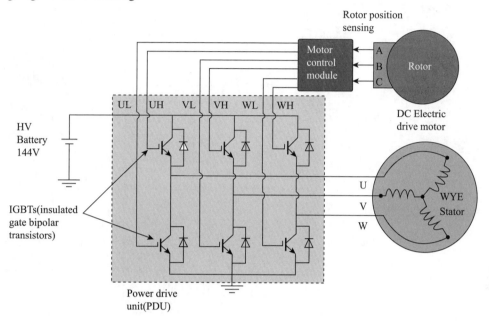

Figure 3.10 A typical Honda PDU controls the current and voltage through the stator windings of the DC motor

3.3.2 Permanent Magnet AC Motor Controller
永磁交流电机控制器

In most hybrid electric vehicles, traction AC motor is controlled as follows:

- The speed of the motor is changed by changing the frequency of the applied current. The speed is synchronized to the frequency so when the frequency is changed, the speed changes.
- The pulse width and voltage is adjusted to change the power output to match the demands of the vehicle for electric assist or propulsion.

In Toyota Prius HEVs, as shown in Figure 3.11, The boost converter is a DC-DC converter witch boosts the nominal voltage of DC 201.6V that is output by the HV battery to the maximum voltage of DC 500V. A DC-DC converter are electronic devices used to transform DC voltage from one level of DC voltage to another higher or lower level, it's central component is a transformer. The IGBT is used to perform the switching control, and the power transistor is controlled by the HV ECU.

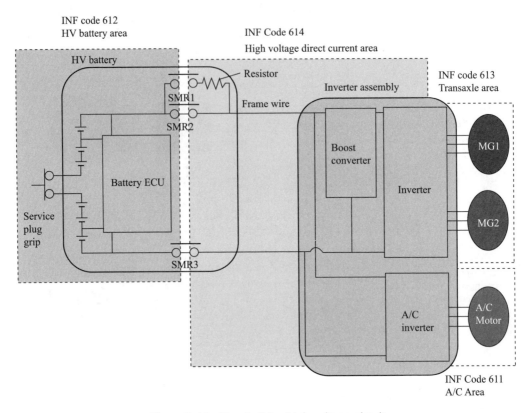

Figure 3.11 Toyota Prius high-voltage circuit

AC motors are powered by inverters. An inverter converts DC power to AC power at the required frequency and amplitude. The inverter converts the high voltage direct current of the battery into three-phase alternating current of MG1 and MG2. When MG1 or MG2 acts as a generator, the inverter converts the alternating current (range from 201.6V to 500V) generated by either of them into direct current. [*2] The boost converter then drops it to DC 201.6V to charge the HV battery. The Toyota Prius' inverter assembly is shown in Figure 3.12.

For Lexus RX 400h, as shown in Figure 3.13, the boost converter is used to transfer the 280V of DC voltage to 650V to drive the motors, and the IGBTs process drive current to the electric drive motor. Main capacitor absorbs voltage spikes that occur when the voltage level is changed in the booster converter.

Figure 3.12 Toyota Prius inverter assembly

Chapter 3
Traction Motors and Controllers

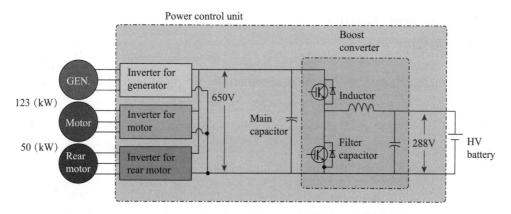

Figure 3.13 Motor controls for Lexus RX 400h 4WD HEVs

New Words		
amplitude	['æmplɪtjuːd]	n. 振幅
collector	[kə'lektə(r)]	n. 集电极
emitter	[ɪ'mɪtə]	n. 发射极
rectify	['rektɪfaɪ]	vt. 整流
spike	[spaɪk]	n. 峰，尖峰，尖端
synchronize	['sɪŋkrənaɪz]	vt. 使同步
transformer	[træns'fɔːmə(r)]	n. 变压器

Phrases and Technical Terms	
boost converter	升压变换器
current driver	电流驱动器
DC-DC converter	直流-直流变换器
driver circuit	驱动电路
electric drive motor	驱动电机
insulated gate bipolar transistor (IGBT)	绝缘栅双极晶体管
inverter assembly	逆变器总成
motor control module (MCM)	电机控制模块
motor controller	电机控制器
power drive unit (PDU)	动力驱动单元
power transistor	功率晶体管
pulse width	脉冲宽度，脉宽

3.4 Service and Testing
维护与测试

Voltage measurements are usually specified to diagnose a DC-DC converter system. A voltage test can indicate if the correct voltages are present when the converter is on and off. A digital multimeter (DMM) that is CAT III-rated should be used.

Safety precautions when working with high-voltage circuits:

- Always follow the manufacturer's safety precautions. High-voltage circuits are usually indicated by orange wiring.
- Never tap into wires in a DC-DC converter circuit to access power or ground for another circuit.
- Never block airflow to a DC-DC converter heat sink.
- Never use a heat sink for a ground connection for a meter, scope, or accessory connection.
- Never connect or disconnect a DC-DC converter while the converter is powered up.
- Never connect a DC-DC converter to a larger-voltage source than specified.

Whenever diagnosing a motor or control fault, use a scan tool and check for any stored diagnostic trouble codes (Table 3.1) and then follow the vehicle manufacturer's recommended pinpoint tests to determine the root cause.

Table 3.1 Generic motor/controller diagnostic trouble codes

DTCs	Meanings
P0A00	Motor electronics coolant temperature sensor circuit
P0A01	Motor electronics coolant temperature sensor circuit range/performance
P0A02	Motor electronics coolant temperature sensor circuit/low
P0A03	Motor electronics coolant temperature sensor circuit/high
P0A04	Motor electronics coolant temperature sensor circuit/intermittent
P0A05	Motor electronics coolant pump control circuit/open
P0A06	Motor electronics coolant pump control circuit/low
P0A07	Motor electronics coolant pump control circuit/high
P0A08	DC-DC converter status circuit/open
P0A09	DC-DC converter status circuit/low
P0A10	DC-DC converter enable circuit/high
P0A11	DC-DC converter enable circuit/open
P0A12	DC-DC converter enable circuit/low
P0A13	DC-DC converter enable circuit/high

Chapter 3
Traction Motors and Controllers

New Words

block	[blɒk]	vt. 阻止
diagnose	['daɪəgnəʊz]	vt. 诊断，判断
indicate	['ɪndɪkeɪt]	vt. 指示，表明
intermittent	[ˌɪntə'mɪtənt]	adj. 间歇的
multimeter	['mʌltɪmiːtə]	n. 万用表
pinpoint	['pɪnpɔɪnt]	adj. 详尽的
precaution	[prɪ'kɔːʃn]	n. 预防，预防措施
scope	[skəʊp]	n. 示波器
specify	['spesɪfaɪ]	vt. 指定；vi. 明确提出
status	['steɪtəs]	n. 地位，情形，状态

Phrases and Technical Terms

diagnostic trouble code	故障码
digital multimeter（DMM）	数字式万用表
enable circuit	使能电路
heat sink	散热片
pinpoint test	详细测试
root cause	根本原因
status circuit	状态电路
tap into	利用

NOTES

*1 The IGBTs are current drivers that send current from the battery pack through the stator windings to energize the stator coils and move the rotor to power the drive wheels.

【句子分析】 句中 that send current from...to power the drive wheels 是 drivers 的定语从句。move 前省略 to，它与 energize 并列。to energize the stator coils and move the rotor to power the drive wheels 是定语从句的状语，说明电流流动的结果。本句的定语从句太长，单独译出。

【参考译文】 IGBT 是电流驱动装置，它们让电流从电池组传送出去，并通过定子绕组，让定子绕组励磁，从而使转子运动，带动驱动轮旋转。

*2 When MG1 or MG2 acts as a generator, the inverter converts the alternating current (range of 201.6V to 500V) generated by either of them into direct current.

【句子分析】 注意句中的搭配 converts... into...（将……转变成……）和做后置定语的分词短语 generated by either of them。

【参考译文】 当 MG1 和 MG2 作为发电机运行时，变换器将它们中的任何一个产生的交流电（电压范围从 201.6V 到 500V）转换为直流电。

Chapter 4

Transmission Systems
传动系统

4.1 Classification of Hybrid Drive
混合动力的分类

4.1.1 Categorize According to the Layout of the Prime Movers
按原动机布置分类

Hybrid drives are drives that have at least two different prime movers and energy accumulators.

According to the layout of the prime movers, hybrid drives can be divided into serial hybrid, parallel hybrid and power-split hybrid (also called series-parallel hybrid) drive as follows.

- Serial hybrid drive (Figure 4.1)

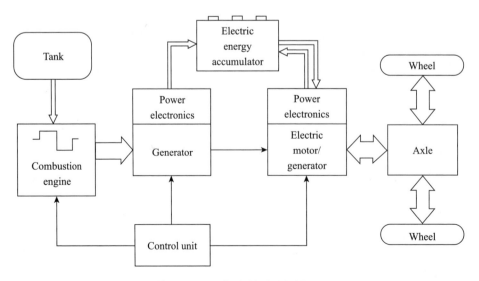

Figure 4.1　Serial hybrid drive

◇ no mechanical coupling of combustion engine and wheels.
◇ mechanical gearbox not mandatory.
◇ a combustion engine, in conjunction with a generator, functions solely as a electricity producer.
◇ two high-performance electric machines (generator + generator/electric motor).

- Parallel hybrid drive (Figure 4.2)
    ◇ both drives can be combined.
    ◇ mechanical gearbox required.
    ◇ only one electric machine is necessary.

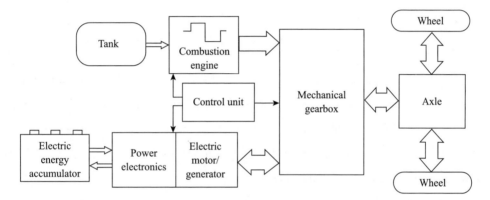

Figure 4.2 Parallel hybrid drive

- Power-split hybrid drive (Figure 4.3)

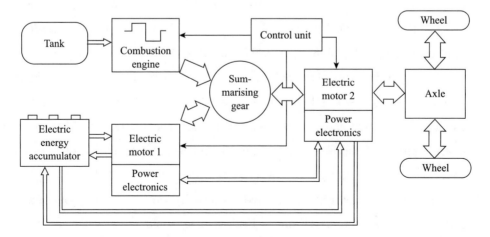

Figure 4.3 Power-split hybrid drive

◇ splitting of the combustion engine power output into mechanical and electric paths.

◇ summarising gear (planetary gear sets) required for the splitting and joining of the mechanical and electric power-paths.

◇ at least two high-performance electric machines are needed.

4.1.2　Categorize by Their Levels of Hybridization　按混动水平分类

PHEV models can also be categorized by their levels of hybridization. Hybridization factor (HF) is a metric used for this purpose and represents the relative value of the power of the electric motor to the total power of the vehicle. Therefore, it can be computed according to

$$HF = \frac{P_{EM}}{P_{EM} + P_{ICE}}$$

where, P_{EM} represents the peak power of the electric motor and P_{ICE} is the peak power of the internal combustion engine. For a conventional ICEV we have HF = 0, while the HF of a BEV is 1, and the hybridization factor of PHEVs ranges between zero and one.

There are different levels of "hybridization" among hybrids on the market. Different vehicle manufacturers use various hybrid technologies.

- Mild hybrid. A mild hybrid, also called a micro-hybrid, usually uses a 42-volt electrical motor and battery package (36-volt batteries, 42-volt charging) and is not capable of using the electric motor to propel the vehicle on its own without help from the internal combustion engine. A mild hybrid system has the advantage of costing less, and saves less fuel compared to a full hybrid vehicle. The fuel savings for a mild type of hybrid design is about 8% to 15%.

- Medium hybrid. A medium hybrid uses 144- to 158-volt batteries. Like a mild hybrid, a typical medium hybrid is not capable of propelling the vehicle from a stop using battery power alone. The fuel savings are about 20% to 25% for medium hybrid systems. Examples of a medium hybrid include Honda Accord, Insight and Civic.

- Full hybrid. A full hybrid, also called a strong hybrid, is able to propel the vehicle using the electric motor (s) alone. Each vehicle manufacturer has made its decision on which hybrid type to implement based on its assessment of the market niche for a particular model. The fuel economy savings are about 30% to 50% for full hybrid systems. Examples of a full or strong hybrid include the Ford Escape SUV, Toyota Prius and Highlander, Lexus RX400h and GS450h.

New Words

hybridization	[ˌhaɪbrɪdaɪˈzeɪʃn]	n. 杂交，杂种培植，配种；杂化
mandatory	[ˈmændətəri]	adj. 强制的
mover	[ˈmuːvə(r)]	n. 原动机，发动机
niche	[nɪtʃ]	n. 壁龛，合适的位置，有利可图的缺口，商机

Phrases and Technical Terms

at least	至少
CE	内燃机
fuel economy	燃料经济性
full hybrid	重度混合动力
hybrid drive	混合动力，混合驱动装置
hybridization factor	混合度
in conjunction with	与……一起
market niche	市场定位，商机
medium hybrid	中度混合动力
micro hybrid	微混合动力
mild hybrid	轻度混合动力
on its own	靠自己
parallel hybrid	并联式混合动力
power-split hybrid	功率分流式混合动力，混联式混合动力
prime mover	原动机，原动力，发动机
serial hybrid	串联式混合动力
series-parallel hybrid	混联式混合动力，功率分流式混合动力
strong hybrid	重度混合动力，强混合动力

4.2 Passenger Car Hybrid Drive
乘用车混合动力传动系统

4.2.1 BMW 6-speed Parallel Hybrid Passenger Car Automatic Gearbox
宝马 6 速并联式混合动力乘用车自动变速器

Operation

The BMW parallel hybrid described in the following as an example (Figure 4.4) is a full hybrid. The basic gear unit in the transmission system is a ZF 6-speed automatic transmission. The "add-on" hybrid module, consisting of an electric machine EM with the two clutches C1 and C2, replaces the torque converter and also takes over its function as moving-off element. By being mounted on the gear input shaft, the electric machine can take over the drive or generator functions with varying power and torque requirements.

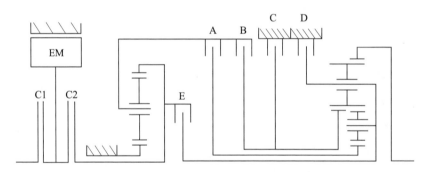

Figure 4.4 6-speed passenger car hybrid automatic transmission as a parallel hybrid with one electric machine (BMW, ZF)

The hybrid functions are implemented in the different operational states represented in Figure 4.5. The directions of the arrows always indicate the direction of' the power flow.

a) Cold start of the CE through the electric machine via clutch C1 (the engine starter may thus be omitted).

b) The vehicle is stationary, the CE runs and loads the electric energy storage unit (electrochemical battery or double-layer capacitors) with the electric machine operated as generator via the closed clutch C1.

c) If the charge state of the energy storage permits it, the CE can be turned off in stationary phases during stop-and-go traffic or at traffic lights (engine start/stop). The on-board power supply is taken over during these phases by the energy storage.

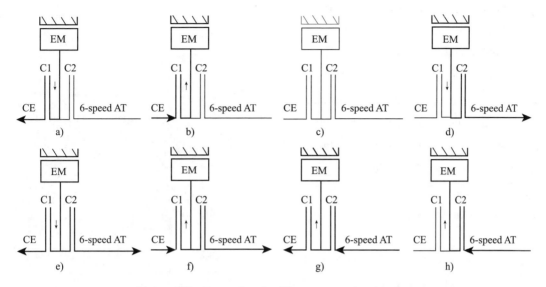

Figure 4.5 Power flow in different operational states

d) Electric moving-off or manoeuvring (CE is off, clutch C1 is open and C2 closed).

e) Starting up the CE at higher driving speeds or given a higher performance demand on the part of the driver via the slipping clutch C1.

f) When the CE has been synchronized, the slip at the clutch C1 is reduced and the CE takes over the drive power. In this operational state, the electric machine can temporarily overlay its torque with that of the engine, as e.g. when boosting or when compensating for the torque of the omitted torque increase of the torque converter.

g) In coasting situations, e.g. driving downhill, the coasting torque can be produced by the generator operation of the electric machine. The coasting energy is thus converted into electric energy and temporarily stored in the energy storage. With a higher level of power, electric energy can be recuperated when braking.

h) The efficiency of the conversion of kinetic energy into electric energy in coasting situations or when braking can be increased given the fact that, in these operational states, the CE along with its drag torque can be uncoupled and switched off due to the opening of the clutch C1 and thus doesn't have to be additionally dragged[*1].

Construction

In comparison to conventional torque converter transmissions, here the torque converter is replaced in its function as moving-off element by the permanent magnet three-phase synchronous motor (PSM), comprising a stator 1 and a rotor 2, as shown in Figure 4.6. The motor is integrated together with the two wet-running multi-plate clutches C1 3 and C2 4 as a hybrid module into the bell-shaped housing, requiring no additional installation space. The separating clutch C1 and the master clutch C2 are engaged and oil-cooled by means of the hydraulic transmission control unit.

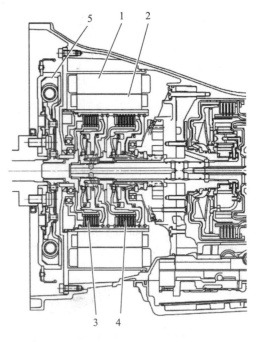

4.2.2 Toyota/Lexus Power-Split Hybrid Transmissions
丰田/雷克萨斯功率分流式混合动力变速器

Operation

Figure 4.6 BMW parallel hybrid 6-speed passenger car automatic gearbox
1—EM stator 2—EM rotor 3—multi-plate clutch C1
4—multi-plate clutch C2 5—dual mass flywheel

While the control system is complex, the basic transaxle of Toyota/Lexus hybrid system is very simple in design as it is built around a single planetary gear set (power-split device) and two electric motor/generators (MG1 and MG2), as shown in Figure 4.7. The power-split device is connected to the IC engine, MG1 and MG2, see Figure 4.8.

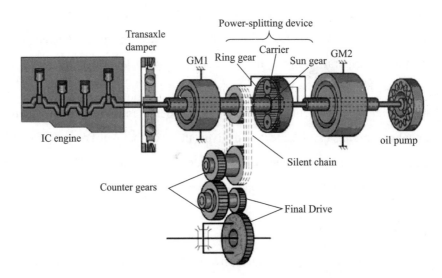

Figure 4.7 The basic transaxle of Toyota/Lexus hybrid system

Chapter 4
Transmission Systems

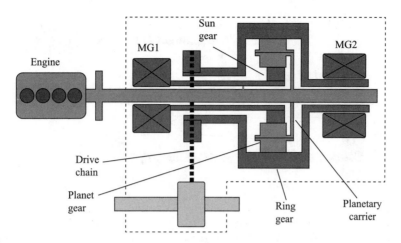

Figure 4.8 The power-split device

• **Vehicle Stopped.** When the vehicle is stopped, nothing is happening with the vehicle drive system. The ICE is shut off, and both electric motors/generators are shut off as well, as shown in Figure 4.9.

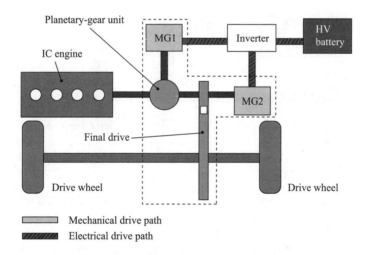

Figure 4.9 When the vehicle is stopped, the ICE is shut off along with both motor/generators

• **Light Acceleration.** When the vehicle is driven at low speeds and light acceleration, it is driven by MG2 alone. See Figure 4.10.

Current from the HV battery is sent through the inverter and on to MG2 to move the vehicle. When the engine is stopped (0 rpm), MG2 is turning forward, and this causes MG1 to turn backward. See Figure 4.8.

• **Normal Driving.** When higher vehicle speeds are required, the ICE must be started so that its output can be combined with that of MG2. See Figure 4.11.

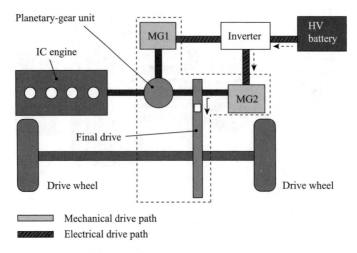

Figure 4. 10 Under light acceleration, electrical power is send to MG2 to move the vehicle

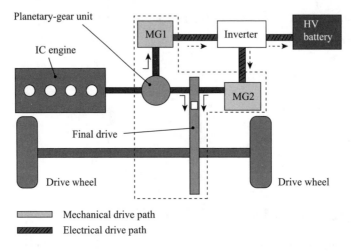

Figure 4. 11 Under normal driving, the IC engine is now running and some of its torque is used to drive MG1. Electricity generated by MG1 is used to power MG2 or recharge the HV battery

The ring gear is already turning clockwise as the vehicle travels in a forward direction. Since the planet carrier (attached to the ICE) is stationary, the sun gear (driven by MG1) is used to drive the planet carrier clockwise and start the ICE. Current from the HV battery is directed through the inverter and operates MG1 as a motor, turning clockwise and spinning the ICE up to 1000 rpm for starting.

Once the ICE is started, MG1 operates as a generator, but turns in the counterclockwise direction. ICE output is now divided or "split" between the drive wheels (ring gear) and MG1 (sun gear). Power generated by MG1 is either directed to MG2 to help move the vehicle or used to recharge the HV battery if necessary.

- Full-Throttle Acceleration and High-Speed Cruise. When greater acceleration is required, both MG2 and the IC engine continue sending torque to the vehicle drive wheels, but MG2 can also receive power from the HV battery to increase its output, as shown in Figure 4.12.

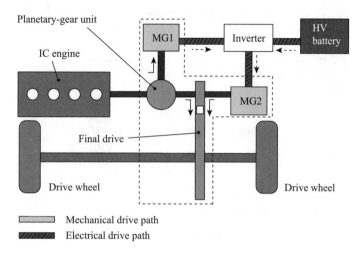

Figure 4.12 During full-throttle acceleration and high-speed cruise, electric power from MG1 is combined with the power from the HV battery to generate greater output from MG2

- Deceleration and Braking. As the vehicle is decelerating or braking, MG2 operates as a generator. The kinetic energy of the vehicle is then converted into electrical energy by MG2. The IC engine and MG1 are shut off, and current from MG2 is sent through the inverter and is then used to recharge the HV battery, as shown in Figure 4.13.

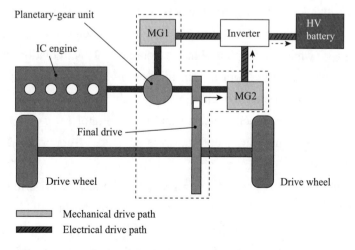

Figure 4.13 During deceleration and braking, MG2 operates as a generator and recharge the HV battery

- Reverse. If reverse is selected, power is sent from the HV battery to the inverter and then on to MG2, as shown in Figure 4.14. MG2 operates in the reverse direction to back up the vehicle, but the other components in the drive system are turned off at this time.

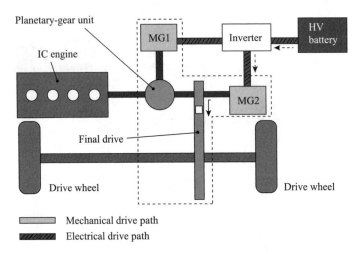

Figure 4.14　During reverse, power is sent from the HV battery to the inverter and then to MG2

Construction

Figure 4.15 and Figure 4.16 show the design of the Toyota/Lexus P310 power-split hybrid transmission with two electric machines. This hybrid transmission with integrated front axle differential is used in SUVs with transverse engines and front-wheel drive.

Both the electric motor and the generator are permanent magnet three-phase synchronous motors (PSM) operated inside the gearbox, i.e. in the oil area. The two electric machines are cooled both via the ATF oil, which conducts their waste heat away through the gearbox housing and into the surrounding area, and via a cooling water jacket around the stators of the electric machines, which is coupled with the cooling water circulation of the vehicle[*2].

A central assembly of this hybrid transmission is the first planetary gearbox, the summarising gear, which couples the engine crankshaft with the output (connected ring gears of the summarising and reduction gears) and the generator (sun gear). In this way, it is possible to exploit the engine power both to drive the gears - supported when necessary by the electric motor - and to drive the generator.

The second planetary gear, the reduction gear, has the task of lowering the speed of the electric motor in the direction of the output and increasing torque. This allows for more compact dimensions for the high-performance electric motor. Moreover, the electric motor is connected to the sun gear, while the ring gear, which is coupled to the ring gear of the summarising gear, represents the output in the direction of the front axle differential. The spider shaft is connected firmly to the gearbox housing.

Chapter 4
Transmission Systems

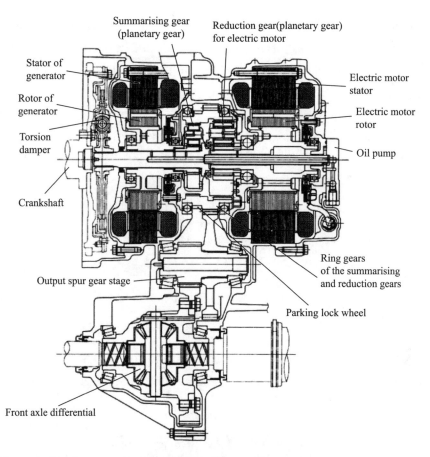

Figure 4.15 Structure drawing of Toyota/Lexus P310 power-split hybrid gearbox

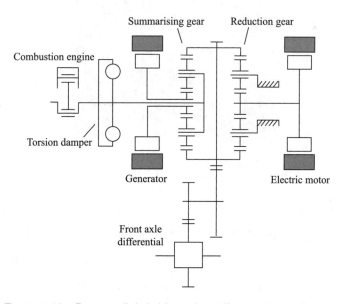

Figure 4.16 Power-split hybrid gearbox (Toyota/Lexus P310)

The powertrain can take on certain properties of an all-wheel drive if the rear axle of the vehicle is electrified by means of a combination of the rear axle differential with an additional third electric machine MGR, as shown in Figure 4.17. This electric machine can be energized from the electric energy accumulator or, when the engine is running, from the electric power path of the generator.

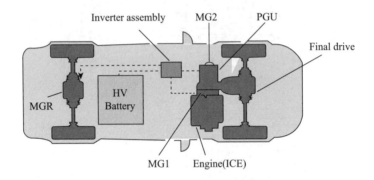

Figure 4.17　An all-wheel drive hybrid drive system

The Toyota P111 power-split hybrid gearbox (used for 2003 Prius) and P112 power-split hybrid gearbox for 2004 & later Prius use chain drive. See Figure 4.18.

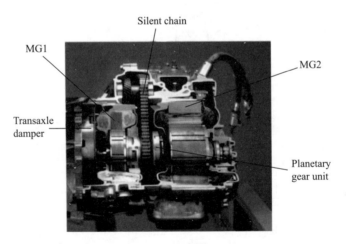

Figure 4.18　The Toyota P111 power-split hybrid gearbox

4.2.3　Ford Escape Hybrid eCVT
福特 Escape 混合动力电控无级变速器

The Ford hybrid uses an electronically controlled continuously variable transmission that includes one planetary gear set. Instead of shifting from one ratio (gear) to the next in steps, the transaxle is designed to function smoothly, without detectable ratio changes. This transaxle design combines the torque from the engine and traction (electric) motor. As a result, the gasoline engine can be shut down at low speeds and light loads to save fuel, while the vehicle is powered solely by the traction motor. The transaxle also routes a portion of the power produced by the engine to a generator.

Operation

The Ford hybrid transaxle operates in one of four modes, as follows:
- Series Mode. When the vehicle is stationary and the ICE is running, the transaxle will enter this mode. The ICE is running to charge the batteries or for climate control reasons. See Figure 4.19.
- Positive Split Mode. During normal operation, the ICE is running and driving the generator motor to produce electricity. Power from the ICE is split between the direct path to the drive wheels and the path through the generator motor. See Figure 4.20.

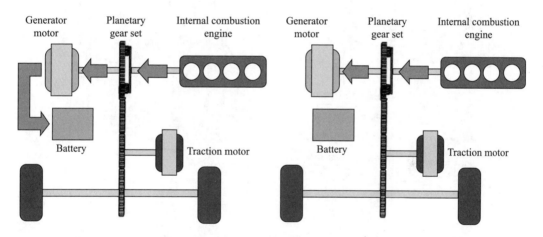

Figure 4.19 Series mode   Figure 4.20 Positive split mode

- Negative Split Mode. This mode is used during highway driving when the ICE has to be on but the HV battery pack does not need to be charged. The generator motor is being used to consume electrical energy to reduce engine speed. The traction motor can operate as a motor or a generator.
- Electric Mode. The vehicle is being propelled using stored electrical energy only using the traction motor. This mode is used in reverse because the ICE cannot deliver reverse torque through the transaxle.

During braking, the traction motor temporarily becomes a generator. The negative torque created by the generator is used to slow the vehicle, reducing the load on the base brakes and recharging the high-voltage battery pack.

Construct

The Ford hybrid transaxle (Figure 4.21) includes the following components: a 36-kW permanent magnet AC generator motor, a 70-kW permanent magnet AC traction motor, a planetary gear set, final drive gears and integrated power electronics/ inverter.

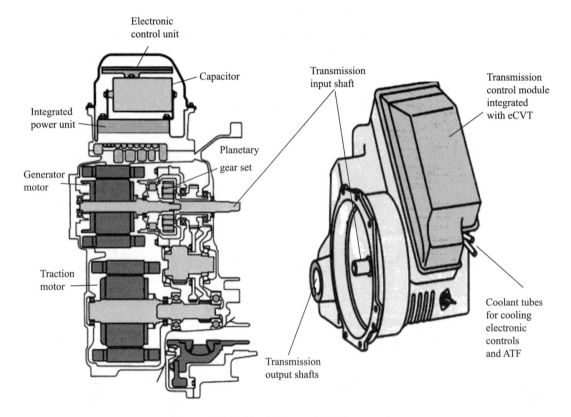

Figure 4.21 Ford Escape hybrid transaxle

4.2.4 Honda Hybrid System 本田混合动力系统

Honda hybrid system is known as Integrated Motor Assist (IMA) (Figure4.22). IMA is a parallel-hybrid configuration that uses a motor-generator located between the ICE and the transmission. The IMA motor (Figure 4.23) is an AC synchronous electric machine that can provide torque assist for moving the vehicle or generate electricity for recharging the HV battery module. All of the electronics for this system are located at the rear of the vehicle, with three power cables running between the IMA motor and the intelligent power unit (IPU).

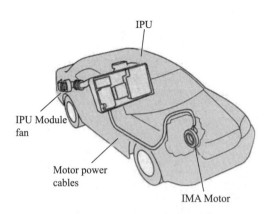

Figure4. 22 Honda hybrid system   Figure 4. 23 Honda hybrid engine assembly

Operation

- Start-up. Under most conditions, Honda hybrid engines are started by the IMA motor, which instantly spins the engine to 1000 rpm.
- Acceleration. During acceleration and other high-load conditions, such as climbing a hill, current from the battery module is converted to alternating current by the MDM (motor drive module) and supplied to the IMA motor, which then functions as a motor. Both the gasoline engine and the electric motor work together to maximize vehicle acceleration.
- Fuel-cut mode. The IMA motor-generator is operated in generation mode. In this mode, the IMA motor is driven by the wheels, generating electricity to be stored in the battery module and slowing the vehicle in the process.
- Decelerating. Regeneration will continue until engine speed falls to about 1000 rpm. In many cases, the gasoline engine will now immediately enter auto idle stop mode.

Construction

The Honda Accord Hybrid automatic transmission is shown in Figure 4. 24. The IMA assembly is located on the end of the crankshaft. The various gears are engaged and disengaged through the application and release of hydraulically operated multiple-disc clutches.

The Honda Accord Hybrid starting with the 2014 model year uses a two-motor hybrid drive system as shown in Figure 4. 25. The two motor/generators are separated by a clutch and each performs two functions:

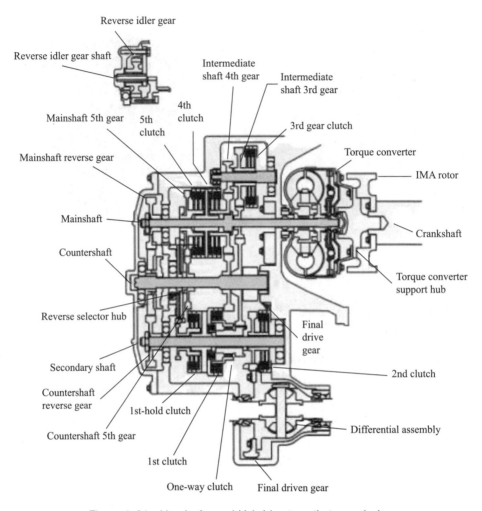

Figure 4.24 Honda Accord Hybrid automatic transmission

- Primary motor/generator. It propels the vehicle and recharges the high-voltage battery during deceleration.
- Secondary motor/generator. It is used to start the gasoline engine and supply electrical energy to the primary motor/generator or charge the high-voltage battery.

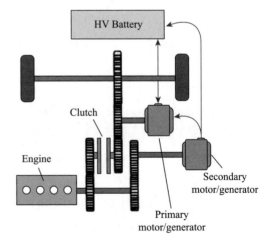

Figure 4.25 Honda Accord Hybrid two-motor hybrid drive system

Chapter 4
Transmission Systems

\<td colspan=3\> New Words		
add-on	[ˈædɒn]	n. 附加物；adj. 附加的
CE		内燃机
coasting	[ˈkəʊstɪŋ]	n. 滑行
comprise	[kəmˈpraɪz]	vt. 包括，由……组成
decelerate	[ˌdiːˈseləreɪt]	vt. & vi. （使）减速
differential	[ˌdɪfəˈrenʃl]	n. 差速器
downhill	[ˌdaʊnˈhɪl]	adv. 向下，如下坡一般
drag	[dræg]	vt. 拖拽，吃力地往前拉；n. 拖，拉，阻力
exploit	[ɪkˈsplɔɪt]	vt. 开采，利用
implement	[ˈɪmplɪmənt]	vt. 实施，执行，实现
kinetic	[kɪˈnetɪk]	adj. 运动的
manoeuvring	[məˈnuːvərɪŋ]	n. 机动，调遣
mount	[maʊnt]	vt. 安装
overlay	[ˌəʊvəˈleɪ]	v. 叠加
phase	[feɪz]	n. 阶段；相
recuperate	[rɪˈkuːpəreɪt]	vi. 再生，回收，复得
situation	[ˌsɪtʃuˈeɪʃn]	n. 情况
starter	[ˈstɑːtə(r)]	n. 起动机
stop-and-go		adj. 不断走走停停的
temporarily	[tempəˈrerɪlɪ]	adv. 暂时地，临时地
transaxle	[trænsˈæksl]	n. 变速驱动桥
uncouple	[ʌnˈkʌpl]	vt. 解开，分开

Phrases and Technical Terms	
all-wheel drive	全轮驱动
along with	与……一起
as e. g.	如
automatic transmission	自动变速器
back up	（使）倒车，倒退
bell-shaped housing	钟形壳

067

(续)

Phrases and Technical Terms	
charge state	荷电状态
continuously variable transmission	机械式无级变速器
drag torque	反拖力矩
driving downhill	下坡
dual mass flywheel	双质量飞轮
energy storage	储能（装置）
front-wheel drive	前轮驱动
gear unit	齿轮机构
given the fact that	鉴于
hybrid module	混合动力模块
in comparison to	与……相比
input shaft	输入轴
integrated motor assist (IMA)	集成化电机辅助
intelligent power unit (IPU)	智能动力单元
kinetic energy	动能
motor drive module (MDM)	电动机驱动模块
moving-off element	移离元件，起步元件
multi-plate clutch	多片离合器
on the part of	由……表现出来的，由……所作出的
overlay...with...	将……与……叠加
planet carrier	行星架
planetary gear set	行星齿轮机构
power supply	供电，电源
spider shaft	行星齿轮轴
summarising gear	合成机构
take over	接管
torque converter	液力变矩器
transmission system	传动系统
water jacket	水套

*1 The efficiency of the conversion of kinetic energy into electric energy in coasting situations or when braking can be increased given the fact that, in these operational states, the CE along with its drag torque can be uncoupled and switched off due to the opening of the clutch C1 and thus doesn't have to be additionally dragged.

【句子分析】 主句的谓语是 can be increased。Given the fact 意为鉴于……，是一个分词短语。后面的 that…是一个同位语从句，先行词为 fact，说明原因。

【参考译文】 在滑行情况下或制动时，动能转换为电能的效率可以提高，因为在这些操作状态下，离合器 C1 的分离可使内燃机 CE 与反拖力矩不耦合而熄火关闭，因此不需要额外拖动而消耗动能。

*2 The two electric machines are cooled both via the ATF oil, which conducts their waste heat away through the gearbox housing and into the surrounding area, and via a cooling water jacket around the stators of the electric machines, which is coupled with the cooling water circulation of the vehicle.

【句子分析】 本句的总体结构是主句后面跟着 both…and…连接的两个并列介词短语，而每个介词短语都有一个定语从句。both…and…连接的两个并列介词短语，译成"既要……，又要……"。第一个定语从句 which conducts…修饰 ATF oil，第二个定语从句 which is coupled with…修饰 cooling water jacket。因为两个定语从句较长，故单独译出。

【参考译文】 这两台电机既要通过 ATF 油冷却又要通过电机定子周围的冷却水套进行冷却。ATF 油通过变速器外壳将废热传送到周围区域，冷却水套与车辆的冷却水循环系统相连接。

Chapter 5

Brief Description to Some Typical EVs
典型电动汽车简介

5.1 Fuel Efficiency Measures
燃料经济性测量

For ICEVs, miles per gallon (MPG) and kilometers per liter are commonly used to represent fuel efficiency rates of vehicles. By incorporating the energy consumption of the PEVs for converting electric energy into motion, miles per gallon equivalent (MPGe) is often referred to as the effective efficiency of the PEVs. MPGe is a measure of distance traveled per unit energy and is calculated as follows.

According to the United States Environmental Protection Agency (EPA), one gallon of gasoline has 115000 BTUs of energy, which is the equivalent of 33.7 kW·h of stored electricity. Therefore, 1 MPGe is approximately the equivalent of 1 mile per 33.7 kW·h or 0.029674 miles per kW·h.

The US EPA calculates the battery-to-wheel MPGe based on the following formula

$$\text{MPGe} = \frac{33705}{E_M}$$

where E_M is wall-to-wheel electrical energy consumed per mile (W·h/mi), which is determined by EPA. This methodology does not consider well-to-wheel life cycle (i.e., generation and transmission of electricity) in order to enable comparing PEVs with ICEVs on battery-to-wheel and tank-to-wheel bases.

In Table 5.1 and Table 5.2, the MPGe values of different BEVs and PHEVs are presented. The associated calculations assume a mixture of 45% of highway driving and 55% of urban driving. For instance, Nissan Leaf's fuel economy is 126 MPGe and 101 MPGe in urban and highway driving, respectively, and their weighted average is 114 MPGe.

Table 5.1 Overview of Battery Electric Vehicles in 2015

Model	AER/mi	MPGe Combined City and HWY	Engine/kW	Battery/kW·h
BMW i3	81	124	125	21
Mercedes B Class	85	84	132	28
Tesla Model S	265	95	300	60
Volkswagen eGolf	83	85	116	24.2
Nissan Leaf	84	114	80	24

Table 5.2 Overview of Plug-in Hybrid Electric Vehicles in 2015

Model	AER/mi	MPGe Combined City and HWY	Engine/kW	Battery/k·Wh
Honda Accord	13	115	124	7
Ford Fusion	20	88	68	7
Toyota Prius	11	95	60	4
Porsche Panamera	16	50	70	9.4
Cadillac ELR	37	82	111	17

New Words

calculation	[ˌkælkjuˈleɪʃn]	n. 计算
consume	[kənˈsjuːm]	vt. 消耗
consumption	[kənˈsʌmpʃn]	n. 消费，消耗
equivalent	[ɪˈkwɪvələnt]	adj. 相当的，等效的
incorporate	[ɪnˈkɔːpəreɪt]	vi. 包含，合并，混合
methodology	[ˌmeθəˈdɒlədʒi]	n. 方法，方法论
present	[ˈpreznt]	n. 呈现

Phrases and Technical Terms

BTU	英国热量单位（=252cal）
kilometers per liter	千米/升
life cycle	生命周期
miles per gallon (MPG)	英里/加仑
miles per gallon equivalent (MPGe)	当量英里/加仑

5.2 Some Typical BEVs
典型纯电动汽车

5.2.1 Tesla Model S 特斯拉 Model S

The Tesla Model S is a full-size all-electric luxury car (Figure 5.1 and Table 5.1), produced by Tesla Motors, and introduced in June 2012. It scored a perfect 5.0 NHTSA automobile safety rating and is the fastest accelerating car currently in production. The Model S ranked as the world's best selling plug-in electric vehicle in 2015.

The United States Environmental Protection Agency (EPA) official range for the 2012 Model S Performance model equipped with an 85 kW·h battery pack is 265 miles (426 km). EPA rates its energy consumption at 237.5 watt-hours per kilometer (38 kW·h/100 mi or 24 kW·h/100 km) for a combined fuel economy of 89 miles per gallon gasoline equivalent (2.64 L/100 km).

Figure 5.1 Tesla Model S

Table 5.1 Tesla Model S P100D main specifications

Model year	2016
Type	plug-in electric vehicle
Power battery	100kW·h, Li-ion
Acceleration	0 – 97 km/h : 2.5s
Range	485 km

The Tesla Model S won awards including the 2013 World Green Car of the Year, 2013 Motor Trend Car of the Year, Automobile magazine's 2013 Car of the Year, Time Magazine Best 25 Inventions of the Year 2012 award and Consumer Reports' top-scoring car ever. In 2015, Car and Driver named the Model S the Car of the Century.

In 2016, Tesla updated the design of the Model S. The 60, 60D, 70, 70D, 75, 75D and 90D versions are available. In August 2016, Tesla introduced the P100D to be the new top-level model. The P100D model has a 100 kW·h battery, a 0 – 60 mph (0 – 97 km/h) time of 2.5 seconds and a driving range of 485km.

5.2.2 Porsche Taycan Turbo and Turbo S
保时捷 Taycan Turbo 与 Turbo S

The Taycan Turbo and Turbo S (Figure 5.2) will go on sale later this year. Both Taycan models are fully electric, sending power to both axles by courtesy of a pair of permanent magnet synchronous electric motors. These are expensive to use, but a compact design, good power density and good heat management outweigh the increased cost. The front axle uses a single-speed gear set with an 8∶1 ratio. The rear axle uses a two-speed transmission, an unusual trait for modern EVs. First gear is used for acceleration. The Taycan shifts around 62 mph, and top speed for both models is 162 mph.

Figure 5.2　Porsche Taycan Turbo and Turbo S

The Turbo and Turbo S both make 616 horsepower. Using an "overboost" function, the Taycan can make up to 670 horsepower, while the Turbo S sends up to 750 horsepower to the wheels. Peak torque is 626 and 774 pound-feet respectively. The torque split is fully variable between the two axles. The Taycan hits 60 mph in 3.0 seconds in the Turbo and 2.6 in the Turbo S. Note that those are both slower than Tesla's numbers for the Model S. The phrase Porsche kept repeating was "repeatable performance" making the point that these cars focused on all-around performance rather than straight-line acceleration. The Porsche Turbo and Turbo S main specifications is listed in Table 5.4.

Table 5.4　Porsche Turbo and Turbo S main specifications

Model year	2020
Type	plug-in electric vehicle
Power battery	93 kW·h, Li-ion
Acceleration	0–97 km/h: 3.0s (Turbo) and 2.6 s (Turbo S)
Range	450 km

Porsche cites a range for the Taycan of 450 kilometers (280 miles). Like most pure EVs, the Taycan's lithium-ion battery pack is mounted on the floor. At the back, the battery forms a "T" shape (Figure 5.3). Total battery capacity is 93 kW·h. The Taycan uses an 800-volt charging system as opposed to the 400-volt setup in most other EVs. This drastically reduces charging times, though the 270 kW·h peak is still limited by the battery. Porsche expects that to improve to 400 – 500 kW·h as technology improves. In optimal conditions, the Taycan can go from 5 percent to 80 percent in 22.5 minutes. That is limited by temperature and the charging infrastructure.

Figure 5.3　Porsche Taycan Lithium-ion Battery Pack

New Words			
drastically	[ˈdrɑːstɪklɪ]	adv.	大幅地
full-size	[ˈfulˈsaɪz]	adj.	正常尺寸的，全尺寸的
hit	[hɪt]	vt.	达到
invention	[ɪnˈvenʃən]	n.	发明
rate	[reɪt]	n.	等级；vt. 定级
specification	[ˌspesɪfɪˈkeɪʃn]	n.	规格

Phrases and Technical Terms	
by courtesy of	蒙……允许
Car of the Year	年度最佳汽车
luxury car	豪华汽车
rank as	可算作……
World Green Car of the Year	世界年度绿色汽车

5.3　Some Typical HEVs
典型混合动力汽车

5.3

5.3.1　Toyota Prius　丰田普锐斯

When the Prius was first released, it was selected as the world's best-engineered

Chapter 5
Brief Description to Some Typical EVs

passenger car for 2001. The car was chosen because it is the first hybrid vehicle that seats four to five people plus their luggage, and it is one of the most economical and environmentally friendly vehicles available. Then in 2004, the second generation Prius won the prestigious Motor Trend Car of the Year award and best-engineered vehicle of 2004.

Figure 5.4 Toyota Prius

The new generation Prius is shown in Figure 5.4. Toyota Prius main specifications are listed in Table 5.5.

Table 5.5 **Toyota Prius main specifications**

Model year	1997–2003	2003–2011	2009–2015	2015–
Hybrid type	Series-parallel	Series-parallel	parallel-parallel	Series-parallel
IC engine	1.5 liter, inline, 4-cyl., 78kW	1.5 liter, inline, 4-cyl., 103kW	1.8 liter, inline, 4-cyl., 133kW	1.8 liter, inline, 4-cyl., 133kW
Traction motor	288V, 29kW	500V, 50kW	650V, 60kW	650V, 53kW
Power battery	NiMH	NiMH	NiMH	NiMH, Li-ion

The innovative features of the Prius are in the design details of the power sources and the power-split device in the hybrid transmission. The Toyota Hybrid System (THS) has two power sources (Figure 5.5): a 1.5 liter petrol engine, developing 42.5 kW at 4000 rpm and a peak torque of 102 N·m at 4000 rpm and a battery-powered permanent magnet synchronous electric motor with a maximum output of 30 kW over the speed range of 940–2000 rpm and peak torque of 305 N·m from standstill to 940 rpm[*1]. The Prius has achieved a remarkably low fuel consumption of 28 km/liter (79.5 mpg or 3.57 litre/100 km).

The petrol engine is the hybrid's main power source. It is a 1.5 liter DOHC 16 valve, 13.5:1 compression ratio, engine with variable valve timing intelligent (VVT-i) and electronic fuel injection, using the highly heat-efficient Miller cycle, that, in turn, is a further development of the high expansion Atkinson cycle. In this cycle the expansion continues for longer period than in the conventional 4-stroke engine, thereby extracting more of the thermal energy of the burning gases than can be achieved in a engine of conventional design[*2].

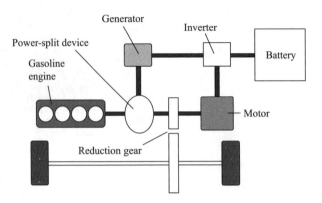

Figure 5.5　Toyota Prius hybrid system

  The power-split device (Figure 5.6) employs a planetary gear system. One of the output shafts of the power split device is linked to the electric generator, while the other is linked to the electric motor and road wheels.

  The complex transmission system, which also includes a reduction gear, is electronically controlled, so that the respective speed of the petrol engine, the electric generator, and the electric motor are held within the optimum performance band. The distribution of the petrol engine's power is determined by such factors as throttle opening, vehicle speed, and state of battery charge.

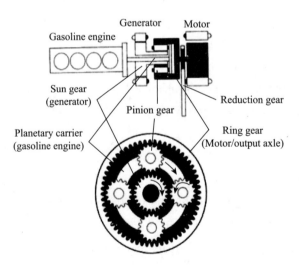

Figure 5.6　The power-split device

  The ECUs keeps the engine operating in a predetermined high torque to maximize fuel economy. The hybrid ECU controls overall drive force by calculating engine output, motor torque and generator drive torque, based on accelerator and shift position. Request values

Chapter 5
Brief Description to Some Typical EVs

sent out are received by other ECUs. The motor ECU controls the inverters to output a 3 phase AC current for desired torque. The engine ECU controls the electronic throttle in accordance with requested output. The braking ECU coordinates braking effort of motor regeneration and mechanical brakes. The battery ECU controls charge rate.

5.3.2 2020 Mercedes-Benz GLC 350e
2020 款梅赛德斯 – 奔驰 GLC 350e

The 350e EQ Power (Figure 5.7 and Table 5.6) has Mercedes-Benz's third-generation plug-in hybrid technology. It combines a turbocharged four-cylinder engine that makes 208 peak horsepower and 258 lb-ft of peak torque with an electric motor that makes 121 horsepower and 325 lb-ft of torque[*3]. In total, the 350e EQ Power is rated at 315 horsepower and 516 lb-ft of torque. Benz estimates it could do zero to 60 mph in 5.6 seconds, improved from 6.2 seconds.

Figure 5.7　Mercedes-Benz 350e EQ Power

Table 5.6　2020 Mercedes-Benz GLC 350e main specifications

Model year	2020
Hybrid type	Plug-in hybrid
IC engine	Turbocharged, 4-cylinder, 208 peak horsepower
Traction motor	121 horsepower
Power battery	13.5 kW · h

Power is put to the ground through Benz's 9G-TRONIC transmission (previously seven-speed) and 4MATIC all-wheel-drive system. The new hybrid design includes the use of a torque converter with an integrated lockup clutch as a starting device, and a second clutch between the gas engine and the electric motor allows for full electric driving.

The most significant change for the 2020 model year is a battery pack upgrade from 8.7 kW · h to 13.5 kW · h. The bigger battery pack allows for an extended electric-only range. A new onboard charger increases charging capacity from 3.6 kW to 7.4 kW.

For 2020, the entire GLC range including the 350e gets a host of upgraded standard features. It now has the new Mercedes-Benz User Experience (MBUX) infotainment system across a 12.3-inch digital instrument cluster and 10.25-inch touch screen multimedia infotainment display, including Android Auto and Apple CarPlay integration. It also has a new-generation touchpad and multifunction steering wheel. Keeping safety in mind, the 350e comes standard with active brake assist, adaptive braking technology, crosswind assist, and attention assist.

5.3.3 2020 Volkswagen Passat GTE 2020 款大众帕萨特 GTE

A mid-life update and up-spec for Volkswagen's Europe-built Passat range brings a plug-in hybrid-electric (PHEV) version — a first for the model — for MY2020. Not for the first time (the Phaeton was one example), VW markets a model in terms of refinement, quality and aesthetics that is arguably very close to being an Audi in all but badge. The latest-generation 8.5 Passat GTE hybrid, built off the company's MQB platform, takes it still closer to its Audi brethren.

Figure 5.8 Passat GTE hybrid

Table 5.7 2020 Volkswagen Passat GTE main specifications

Model year	2020
Hybrid type	plug-in hybrid
IC engine	148-hp 1.4-liter turbocharged gasoline
Traction motor	85 kW (114 hp)
Power battery	13 kW·h

The GTE may seem to indicate a sporty GT version, but it is not that; however, the nomenclature could reasonably stand for Great Technology and Electrified. The plug-in hybrid is quite brisk, 0-to-62 mph (100 km/h) runs take 7.4 sec and top speed is 138 mph (222 km/h). Curb weight is 1730 kg (3814 lb).

The electric motor and 148-hp (110-kW) 1.4-L turbocharged gasoline engine work together with linear smoothness; Maximum torque is 243 lb-ft (330 N·m). Peak electrical power is quoted at 85 kW (114 hp); battery capacity is 13 kW·h and combined drive cycle electric consumption is 165 W·h/km, with electric-only range a practical 35 miles (56 km).

With a light touch on the accelerator, the electric motor will comfortably waft the car to national speed limits from standstill. The GTE's powertrain drives through a 6-speed DSG gearbox, although other 2020 Passats get a 7-speed. The DSG incorporates a third disengagement clutch that decouples the ICE whenever possible to make best use of kinetic energy.

On the cruise, the ICE is quiet and MacPherson strut front, multi-link rear suspension make for a good ride and handling compromise. Infotainment now includes New Travel Assist, making the latest Passat the first VW that can be driven at up to 130 mph (209 km/h) in assisted-driving mode.

5.3.4　MAN Hybrid Bus　曼混合动力客车

A low floor city bus (Figure 5.9) developed by a joint venture between MAN and Voith uses a diesel-electric series hybrid system (Figure 5.10 and Table 5.8). The bus is 12 metres long and designed to carry 98 passengers at a maximum speed of 70 kph. No steps are involved at any of the entrances which lead directly to a completely level deck height of between 317 and 340 mm.

Figure 5.9　A MAN series hybrid bus

Table 5.8　MAN hybrid bus main specifications

Hybrid type	Series hybrid
IC engine	127 kW diesel
Generator	135 kW
Traction motor	Permanent magnet synchronous wheel motors, 57 kW

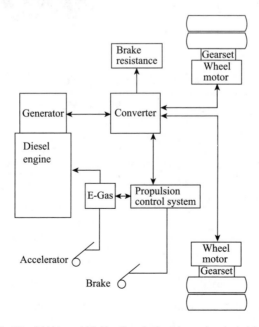

Figure 5.10　MAN and Voith diesel-electric series hybrid system

The rear mounted horizontally positioned diesel engine allows fitment of a bench seat at the rear of the bus; it drives a generator with only electrical connection to the Voith transverse-flux wheel motors which drive the wheels through two-stage hub-reduction gear sets.

The diesel is rated at 127 kW and the generator at 135 kW. The controller is of the IGBT converter type, and provides a differential action to the wheel motors on cornering. Permanent magnet synchronous wheel motors are rated at 57 kW and have a maximum speed of 2500 r/min. The bus has a water cooling system for its generator, converters and wheel motors.

5.3.5 Mitsubishi Hybrid Truck 三菱混合动力货车

Mitsubishi have recently developed a heavier municipal version of the light hybrid truck launched in 1995, it's main specifications listed in the Table 5.9. Because added cost limited market acceptance of the lighter canter-based hybrid, the decision to build a heavier municipal version (Figure 5.11) was taken on the grounds of low noise, and greatly reduced emissions, which made the vehicle attractive for city-centre operation, and a lift-platform version being particularly popular[*4]. The hydraulic pump for operating auxiliaries such as a lift platform is electric motor driven, with the benefit of near silent operation.

Figure 5.11 Mitsubishi hybrid truck

Table 5.9 Mitsubishi hybrid truck main specifications

Hybrid type	Series hybrid
IC engine	1.8 liter, 127 kW diesel
Generator	220 – 360V, 30 kW
Traction motor	288V, 55 kW, induction type
Power battery	lead – acid

Series hybrid mode (Figure 5.12) was chosen first, because the engine is used solely for power generation and so can be operated in a peak efficiency speed band and secondly, since the engine is isolated from the drive system, it results in a simpler and more flexible drive-system layout with greater freedom for hydraulic equipment mounting.

Chapter 5
Brief Description to Some Typical EVs

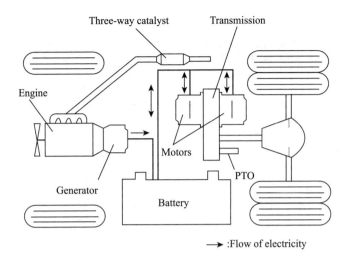

Figure 5.12 Series hybrid system

When the battery has high SOC the vehicle operates exclusively in battery mode. At less than 65% SOC the power-generating engine starts and hybrid mode is invoked; when 70% SOC is achieved again the vehicle reverts to battery operation. Provision is also made to inhibit hybrid operation until 30% SOC is reached so silent and zero emission night-time, or in-tunnel, operation is made possible. In hybrid mode SOC is maintained at 65% – 70%, at which point the generated power, from the generator, and the regenerative power, from the motor, provide sufficient charging.

The overall package layout is shown in Figure 5.11; dimensions are 5.78 m long, 1.88 m wide and 3.35 m high, with a wheelbase of 2.5 m. Gross vehicle weight is 6.965 tonnes and tyre size 205/85R16.

The petrol engine is a 16 valve unit of 1834 ml. The generator has a maximum output of 30 kW at 3500 rpm; it operates at 220 – 360 V and weighs 70 kg. The motors, of 55 kW, are of the induction type and each develop 150 N·m at 3500 rpm, rated voltage being 288 V. Lead—acid traction batteries are employed, 24 units each weighing 25 kg and having 65 A·h capacity at a 5 hour rate. The simple two speed transmission has a PTO for driving the hydraulic pump and reverse motion is achieved by altering the rotation of the electric motor.

New Words		
accelerator	[ək'seləreɪtə(r)]	n. 加速器，节气门
aesthetics	[iːs'θetɪks]	n. 美学
arguably	['ɑːgjuəbli]	adv. 可以说

(续)

New Words		
badge	[bædʒ]	n. 徽章，标记
brisk	[brɪsk]	adj. 快的；轻快的
coordinate	[kəʊˈɔːdɪneɪt]	vi. 协调
crosswind	[ˈkrɒswɪnd]	n. 侧风
cylinder	[ˈsɪlɪndə(r)]	n. 圆筒，气缸
decouple	[diˈkʌpl]	vt. 分离，解耦
disengagement	[ˈdɪsɪnˈgeɪdʒmənt]	n. 脱离，分离
estimate	[ˈestɪmət]	n. & vt. 估计，估算
exclusively	[ɪkˈskluːsɪvlɪ]	adv. 唯一
extract	[ˈekstrækt]	v. 提取，提炼
infotainment	[ˌɪnfəʊˈteɪnmənt]	n. 信息娱乐片
innovative	[ˈɪnəveɪtɪv]	adj. 革新的；创新的
invoke	[ɪnˈvəʊk]	vi. 恳求，实行
isolate	[ˈaɪsəleɪt]	vi. 隔离
municipal	[mjuːˈnɪsɪpl]	adj. 市政的
nomenclature	[nəˈmenklətʃə(r)]	n. 命名
prestigious	[preˈstɪdʒəs]	adj. 受尊敬的，有声望的
revert	[rɪˈvɜːt]	vi. 恢复
smoothness	[smuːðnəs]	n. 平滑；流畅
touchpad	[ˈtʌtʃpæd]	n. 触摸板
turbocharge	[ˈtɜːbəʊtʃɑːdʒ]	vt. 用涡轮给（发动机）增压
waft	[wɒft]	vt. 吹送，使飘荡
wheelbase	[ˈwiːlbeɪs]	n. 轴距

Phrases and Technical Terms	
bench seat	长条座椅
braking effort	制动力
compression ratio	压缩比
curb weight	整备质量

Chapter 5
Brief Description to Some Typical EVs

(续)

Phrases and Technical Terms	
drive force	驱动力
DSG gearbox	双离合变速器
electronic fuel injection	电子控制燃料喷射
electronic throttle	电子节气门
fuel consumption	耗油率，燃料消耗
hub-reduction gear set	轮毂减速机构
in accordance with	按照
in all but	除了
instrument cluster	组合仪表
joint venture	合资企业
lockup clutch	锁止离合器
make best use of	充分利用
Miller cycle	米勒循环
multimedia infotainment display	多媒体信息娱乐显示器
on the grounds of	以……为理由
petrol engine	汽油机
starting device	起步装置
steering wheel	转向盘
thermal energy	热能
touch screen	触摸屏
variable valve timing intelligent	智能型可变气门定时
wheel motor	车轮电机

NOTES

*1 The Toyota Hybrid System (THS) has two power sources (Figure 5.5): a 1.5 liter petrol engine, developing 42.5 kW at 4000 rpm and a peak torque of 102 N·m at 4000 rpm and a battery-powered permanent magnet synchronous electric motor with a maximum output of 30 kW over the speed range of 940 – 2000 rpm and peak torque of 305 N·m from standstill to 940 rpm.

【句子分析】这虽然是一个简单句，但是句子很长。two power sources (Figure 5.5) 之后是两个并列的名词短语：a 1.5 liter petrol engine 和 a battery-powered permanent magnet synchronous electric motor。这两个短语之后的 developing…分词短语和 with…介词短语分别做它们的后置定语。

【参考译文】 丰田混合动力系统（THS）有两个动力源（图5.5）：一个是1.5L汽油机，另一个是电池供电的永磁同步电机。汽油机在4000 r/min 时产生42.5kW 功率和102N·m 的峰值转矩；电动机在940~2000 r/min 的转速范围内产生30 kW 的最大输出；从静止到940 r/min，产生305N·m 的峰值转矩。

*2 In this cycle the expansion continues for longer period than in the conventional 4-stroke engine, thereby extracting more of the thermal energy of the burning gases than can be achieved in a engine of conventional design.

【句子分析】 本句是一个简单句，只是在 for…介词短语和 extracting… 分词短语中分别使用了比较级 longer…than…和 more…than…。

【参考译文】 在这种循环中，膨胀期比传统的四冲程发动机更长，从而能从燃烧气体中提取出比传统设计的发动机（能够提取的）更多的热能。

*3 It combines a turbocharged four-cylinder engine that makes 208 peak horsepower and 258 lb-ft of peak torque with an electric motor that makes 121 horsepower and 325 lb-ft of torque.

【句子分析】 首先应注意到 combine…with…固定搭配（将……与……相结合），其次 combine + 宾语 + with + 宾语中的两个宾语都有一个定语从句。

【参考译文】 它将涡轮增压四缸发动机与电动机相结合，其中发动机产生208hp 的峰值功率和258lb·ft 的峰值转矩，电动机产生121hp 的功率和325lb·ft 的转矩。

*4 Because added cost limited market acceptance of the lighter Canter-based hybrid, the decision to build a heavier municipal version (Figure 5.12) was taken on the grounds of low noise, and greatly reduced emissions, which made the vehicle attractive for city-centre operation, and a lift-platform version being particularly popular.

【句子分析】 句首 Because…是一个原因状语从句。on the grounds of…（根据，考虑到）短语较为复杂：low noise 与 greatly reduced emissions 并列，并且后面有一个定语从句；a lift-platform version being particularly popular 是一个动名词复合结构（说明升降平台车型受欢迎的事实）与 low noise and greatly reduced emissions 并列，共同作为短语介词 on the grounds of 的宾语。

【参考译文】 由于增加的成本限制了以前这款基于 Canter 轻型货车的混合动力汽车的市场接受度，但考虑到低噪声和大幅降低排放使该车对市内作业有吸引力，并且升降平台车型也特别受欢迎，所以决定制造一种较重的市政版本混合动力货车（图5.12）。

Chapter 6

Trouble Diagnosis and Service of Electric Vehicles
电动汽车故障诊断与维护

6.1 General Trouble Diagnosis Procedure and Safety Equipments
一般故障诊断程序和安全设备

6.1.1 Safety Equipments 安全设备

6.1

All electric vehicles and hybrid electric vehicles use high-voltage circuits that if touched with an unprotected hand could cause serious burns or even death[*1]. High-voltage cables are identified by color of the plastic conduit and include blue or yellow (42 volts), or orange (144 to 600 volts or higher). The safety equipments must be used in the servicing and repairing the HV circuits. These equipments include:

- Rubber gloves. Be sure that high-voltage lineman's gloves are available, before working on the high-voltage system of a hybrid electric vehicle. The Occupational Safety and Health Administration (OSHA) requirements specify that the high-voltage gloves get inspected every six months by a qualified glove inspection laboratory. Use an outer leather glove to protect the high-voltage rubber gloves. Remember that the gloves always are inspected carefully before each use.
- Eye protection. When testing for high voltage, wear an eye protection. If the high-voltage system has not been powered down or has not had the high-voltage system disabled, a shock hazard is always possible. Even when the high-voltage system has been disconnected, there is still high voltage in the HV battery box. Some vehicle manufacturers specify that full face shields be worn instead of safety glasses when working with high-voltage circuits or components.
- CAT Ⅲ digital multimeter. This meter is required for making measurements on hybrid electric vehicle high-voltage systems.
- Safety cones. Ford requires that cones be placed at the four corners of any hybrid

electric vehicle when service work on the high-voltage system is being performed. They are used to establish a safety zone around the vehicles so that other technicians will know that a possible shock hazard may be present.
- Fiberglass pole. Ford requires that a ten-foot insulated fiberglass pole be available outside the safety zone to be used to pull a technician away from the vehicle in the unlikely event of an accident where the technician is shocked or electrocuted[*2].

6.1.2 Testing Equipments and Diagnostic Procedures
测试设备与诊断程序

- Scan tools. Although some aftermarket scan tools can access hybrid PIDs and DTCs and perform some bidirectional tests, there is nothing that outperforms the factory scan tool for the specific vehicle. Toyota's Diagnostic Tester (Figure 6.1) will access all available vehicle information and perform all diagnostic testing on the Toyota hybrid system.
- Insulation tester. When testing circuit voltage and loss of insulation, an electrical insulation tester such as the Fluke 1587 (Figure 6.2) can be used.

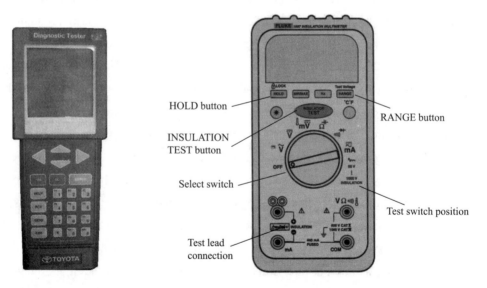

Figure 6.1 Toyota's Diagnostic Tester   Figure 6.2 Fluke 1587 Tester

- General diagnostic procedure. Hybrid electric vehicles should be diagnosed according to following diagnostic procedures.

  Step 1: Verify the customer concern.

  Step 2: Check for diagnostic trouble codes (DTCs).

Step 3: Perform a thorough visual inspection. If a DTC is stored, carefully inspect those areas that might be the cause of the trouble code.

Step 4: Check for technical service bulletins (TSBs) that may relate to the customer concern.

Step 5: Follow service information specified steps and procedures. This could include checking scan tool data for sensors or values that are not within normal range.

Step 6: Determine and repair the root cause of the problem.

Step 7: Verify the repair and clear any stored diagnostic trouble codes unless in an emission testing area.

If in an emission test area, drive the vehicle until the powertrain control module (PCM) passes the fault and turns off the malfunction indicator lamp thereby allowing the vehicle to pass the inspection.

Step 8: Complete the work order and record the "three Cs" (complaint, cause, and correction).

6.1.3 The Leak Monitoring and Testing of Loss of Insulation
漏电监测与绝缘损耗的测试

In the hybrid system, the voltage on the body will be monitored. A high voltage leaking to ground will set a diagnostic trouble code that includes the location of the fault. The high-voltage source will be disconnected if such a fault is found. This type of fault is called a loss of insulation (LOI).

A special tester, such as the Fluke model 1587 (Figure 6.2) is required to test if any of the high-voltage circuits are making contact with the body or ground of the vehicle. To test for electrical continuity between the high-voltage wires or components and the body of the vehicle, test the circuit with a high-voltage ohmmeter that measures megaohms, and perform the following steps.

Step 1: Disable the HV system by removing the safety switch, and allow time for the capacitors to discharge, usually 10 to 20 minutes. Measure the high voltage with a voltmeter to check that the capacitor voltage is zero.

Step 2: Use diagnostic trouble codes and use a vehicle-specific electrical schematic to identify the problem area.

Step 3: To test the power cables from the battery pack to the inverter/converter assembly, for example, disconnect both ends of the cable.

Step 4: The insulation tester applies a high voltage to test the insulation resistance value. Select the 1000-volt scale. Press and hold the "insulation test" button (Figure 6.2) for two seconds to perform the test and the meter will display the measured resistance.

New Words		
bulletin	['bulətɪn]	n. 公告，公报
conduit	['kɒndjuɪt]	n. 导管
continuity	[ˌkɒntɪ'njuːəti]	n. 连续性，连通
disable	[dɪs'eɪbl]	vt. 使无能力，使残废
electrocute	[ɪ'lektrəkjuːt]	vt. 触电致死
lineman	['laɪnmən]	n. 架线兵，线路工人，线务员
megaohm	['megəʊm]	n. 兆欧
ohmmeter	['əʊmmiːtə(r)]	n. 欧姆表
outperform	[ˌaʊtpə'fɔːm]	vt. 胜过
qualified	['kwɒlɪfaɪd]	adj. 有资格的
scale	[skeɪl]	n. 刻度
unprotected	[ˌʌnprə'tektɪd]	adj. 无保护的
verify	['verɪfaɪ]	vt. 核实，验证，证明

Phrases and Technical Terms	
electrical schematic	电气原理图，电气简图
fiberglass pole	玻璃纤维杆
full face shield	全面罩
insulation resistance	绝缘电阻
loss of insulation	绝缘损耗
power down	断电，掉电
safety glasses	安全眼镜
service information specified step	维修信息所规定的步骤
shock hazard	电击危险
technical service bulletin (TSB)	技术服务公报
work order	工作单，工作通知单，工作订单

6.2 Toyota Prius Hybrid Trouble Diagnosis
丰田普锐斯混合动力汽车故障诊断

6.2.1 General Diagnostic Flow and HV System Components Service Safety
一般诊断流程及高压系统组件的维护安全

General Diagnostic Flow

When diagnosing the Prius, follow the diagnostic procedures below.

Step 1: What warning lights are ON? (Critical Information)

Step 2: What is the customer's complaint?

Step 3: What is the condition of the vehicle?

Step 4: Do steps 1-3 agree with each other?

Step 5: Always use "ALL CODES" and print DTCs from each ECU.

Step 6: For multiple DTCs, check the occurrence order.

Step 7: What power source was affected first?

Step 8: How were the other power sources or systems affected?

Step 9: Isolate the system affected first.

Step 10: Always print Freeze Frame Data.

HV system components service safety

Before and during high-voltage system service and repair, be sure to perform following procedures:

- Always wear high-voltage insulated gloves.
- Remove the key from the ignition. If the vehicle is equipped with a smart key, turn the smart key system OFF.
- Always Disconnect the negative (-) terminal cable from the auxiliary battery before removing the high-voltage service plug.
- Remove the service plug and do not make any repairs for five minutes.
- Always use a DVOM to confirm that high-voltage circuits have 0V before performing any service operation.
- Always confirm that you have the service plug in your pocket before performing any service operations.
- Always use the repair manual diagnostic procedures.
- Always assume that high-voltage circuits are energized.
- Remember that removal of the service plug does not disable the individual high-voltage batteries.

6.2.2 Position of the Main Toyota Prius Hybrid Components
丰田普锐斯混合动力系统主要零部件的位置

The main components of the Toyota Prius hybrid system are IC engine, motor generator 1 (MG1), motor generator 2 (MG2), planetary gear set, inverter, HV battery, and HV ECU, as shown in Figure 6.3.

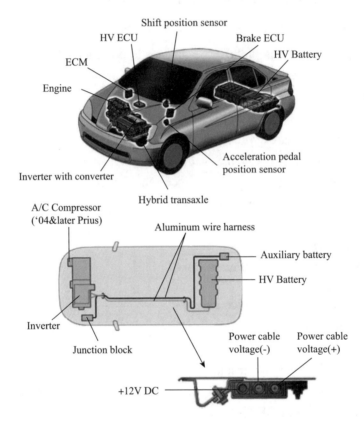

Figure 6.3　The main components of the Toyota Prius hybrid system

6.2.3 The Diagnosis of Toyota Prius Hybrid HV Battery System
丰田普锐斯混合动力高压电池系统诊断

Battery Pack Components

In the battery pack, six nickel metal hydride type 1.2V cells are connected in series to form one module, therefore, one module equals 7.2 volts, 38 modules were installed in series producing 273.6V. In the 2004 and later Prius, 28 modules are connected for a rated voltage of 201.6V.

Chapter 6
Trouble Diagnosis and Service of Electric Vehicles

Prius battery pack contains battery modules, wiring, system main relay (SMR), computer, a manual disconnect service plug, and a strong metal box to contain every thing, as shown in Figure 6.4.

The battery ECU calculates the SOC of the HV battery based on voltage, current and temperature. It then sends the results to the HV ECU. The SMR (Figure 6.5) connects and disconnects the power source of the high-voltage circuit on command from the HV ECU (Figure 6.5). As a result, the proper charge and discharge control is performed. This system also controls the battery blower motor controller in order to maintain a proper temperature at the HV battery assembly.

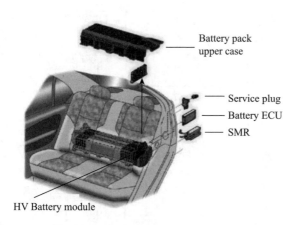

Figure 6.4 The position and components of HV battery pack

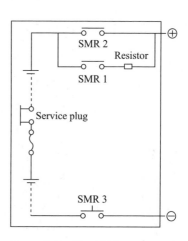

Figure 6.5 The HV battery pack connecting circuit

HV Battery Diagnosis

Since the battery modules are all connected in series, a poor connection at any of the modules can lead to HV battery failure. For this reason, cleanliness of the connections and proper torque on the module fasteners is critical with these battery designs.

A factory scan tool can be used for diagnosing problems that may be related to the high-voltage battery. Toyota high-voltage battery packs have a special wiring harness that allows measurement of the voltage available across pairs of battery modules. These voltage readings can be read as parameter identification (PID) on a scan tool. If the onboard computer recognizes a problem in a module, wiring, or anything that could cause a potential problem, the MIL is illuminated, a code is set, and a freeze frame is stored. The battery pack may be limited in its power output or charging capacity and, as a last resort, the vehicle may be shut down.

Using the hand-held tester, you can read the value of the switches, sensors, actuators and so on without parts removal. Diagnose the HV battery pack using the tester as the

following steps:
- Connect the hand-held tester to the DLC3.
- Turn the power switch ON (IG).
- Turn the hand-held tester ON.
- On the hand-held tester, enter the following menus: DIAGNOSIS / ENHANCED OBD II / HV ECU.
- Select DTC INFO, Read the DTCs, FREEZE FRAME data (Figure 6.6) and the INFORMATION CODEs (Figure 6.7).

The DTCs of the HV battery pack is listed in Table 6.1.

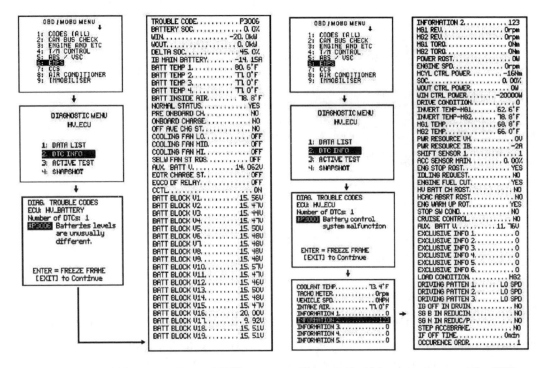

Figure 6.6 Using a tester, read DTCs and FREEZE FRAME data

Figure 6.7 Using a tester, read the DTCs and INFORMATION CODEs

Table 6.1 Toyota Prius Hybrid HV Battery System DTCs (2001 – 2003 Prius)

DTC	Description
DTC P3006 Battery SOC Uneven	The charging rate of each battery is monitored through the battery voltage detection line Drive the vehicle under load while viewing the Min/Max voltage on the Diagnostic Tester. For example, drive up a steep hill very slowly. This kind of load stresses the battery and will allow detection of weak modules If P3006 is the only DTC, refer to the Repair Manual to do a stall test. Monitor the swing and the difference in voltage between the data MAX V and MIN V

Chapter 6
Trouble Diagnosis and Service of Electric Vehicles

（续）

DTC	Description
DTC P3076 Abnormal Battery Cooling Fan Air Flow	If foreign matter clogs the duct, the HV battery might not be able to cool sufficiently. Insufficient cooling will cause the output control warning light to illuminate and may cause DTC P3076 A flesh air duct permits the flow of cooling air when the vehicle is stopped after driving. When washing the car, do not allow large quantities of water to enter the duct

6.2.4 The Diagnosis of Toyota Prius Hybrid Control System
丰田普锐斯混合动力控制系统诊断

Reading Diagnostic Trouble Codes and Information

The procedures to read the DTCs and freeze frame data has described in the previous HV Battery Diagnosis section. Information Codes are some three-digit subset of codes that provide data pertaining to HV ECU DTCs. They provide additional information and freeze frame data to help diagnose the vehicle's condition.

The diagnostic trouble codes of Toyota Prius hybrid control system are listed in the Table 6.2.

Table 6.2　Toyota Prius Hybrid HV Control System DTCs

DTC	Description
DTC P0A4B Generator Position Sensor Circuit (2004 & later Prius)	DTC P0A4B will set when the HV ECU detects output signals that are out of normal range or specification concluding that there is a malfunction of the generator resolver (speed sensor) The following Information Codes can help isolate the problem: • 253 – Interphase short in resolver circuit • 513 – Resolver output is out of range • 255 – Open or short in resolver circuit
DTC P1525 Resoiver Malfunction (2001 & 2003 Prius)	DTC P1525 will set when vehicle speed signals are not input from the resolver (speed sensor) for 16 seconds or more while running at a speed of 20km/h or more. The trouble areas could include the ECM, HV ECU or wire harness
DTC P3120 HV Transaxle Malfunction (2004 & later Prius)	The HV ECU checks the energy balance and detects an abnormality if the magnetism in the motor or generator greatly decreases There are many Information Codes associated with this DTC. Refer to the Repair Manual

DTC	Description
DTC P3125 Converter & Inverter assembly Malfunction	If the vehicle is being driven with a DC-DC converter malfunction the voltage of the auxiliary battery will drop and it will be impossible to continue driving. Therefore, the HV ECU checks the operation of the DC-DC converter and provides a warning to the driver if a malfunction is detected. DTC P3125 will be stored
DTC P3000 HV Battery Malfunction	The HV ECU warns the driver and performs the fail-safe control when an abnormal signal is received from the battery ECU If Information Codes 123 or 125 are output, check and repair the applicable DTC. After repairs, record the DTC of the HV ECU, Freeze Frame data, and Operation History. Then clear the DTC and check one more time after starting the system again, (READY light ON) If information Code 388 is output, check for other Information Codes. Check and repair applicable codes. After that, confirm that there is sufficient gasoline to crank the engine If Information Code 389 is output, check for other Information Codes. Check and repair applicable codes. After that, replace the main battery and crank the engine
DTC P3009 Insulation Leak Detected	DTC P3009 sets when there is a leak in the high-voltage system insulation, which may seriously harm the human body. (Insulation resistance of the power cable is 100 k ohms or less.) If no defect is identified at inspection, entry of foreign matter or water into the battery assembly or converter and inverter assembly may be the possible cause. Use a megger tester to measure the insulation resistance between the power cable and body ground DTC P3009 can alert you to a short circuit in several, different areas of the high-voltage system. The information code retrieved with the DTC helps you pinpoint the exact area of the short circuit. The diagram below shows the specific circuits associated with each of the following information codes: • 526 – Vehicle Insulation Resistance Reduction • 611 – A/C Area • 612 – HV Battery Area • 613 – Transaxle Area • 614 – High voltage DC Area
DTC P3101 Engine System Malfunction (2001 – 2003 Prius)	The HV ECU performs the fail-safe control when the ECM detects an error, which will affect the THS control. Information Codes 204, 205, and 238 may set with this DTC Information Code 204 detects an abnormal signal from the ECM (abnormal engine output). Information Code 205 detects an abnormal signal from the ECM (engine unable to start). Information Code 238 detects when the engine does not start when cranked. If this code is output, investigate what has increased revolution resistance in the transaxle or engine. Check the engine and transaxle lubrication systems, check the engine and transaxle coolant and check for any mechanical breakdowns in the engine and transaxle

Chapter 6
Trouble Diagnosis and Service of Electric Vehicles

(续)

DTC	Description
DTC P3115 System Main Relay Malfunction	The HV ECU checks that the system main relay (No. 1, No. 2, No. 3) is operating normally and detects a malfunction. Information Codes 224 – 229 may be present (Refer to the Repair Manual for each description) Confirm that there is no open circuit in the wire harness. If battery voltage is always applied to the HV ECU Cont 1, Cont 2 and Cont 3 terminals with ignition ON (READY light OFF), the system main relay has a +B short

Accessing Operation History Data

Sometimes symptoms caused by the customer's driving habits may be mistaken for problems in the Prius. Operation History Data can be used for explaining that these symptoms may not indicate problems. It also can be used to view the driving patterns of the customer so that the concern can be diagnosed and fixed.

To view operation history data, the diagnostic tester is operated as follows:

- Connect the diagnostic tester to the DLC3.
- Turn the power switch ON (IG).
- Enter the following menus (Figure 6.8):
  DIAGNOSIS / ENHANCED OBD II → HV ECU → DATA LIST.
- Select the menu to view the number of special operations or controls that have been affected. See Figure 6.8.

Example of diagnostic tester displays is shown in the Table 6.3. For more operation history data, refer to the Appendix 1 at the back of this book.

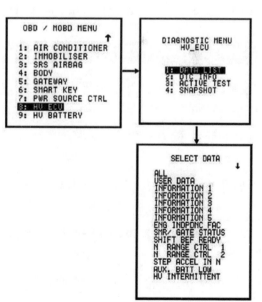

Figure 6.8 Accessing operation history data

Table 6.3 Operation history data

Hand-held tester display	Count condition
STEP ACCEL IN N	Accelerator pedal depressed in N posrtion
AUX. BATTLOW	Auxliary battery voltage below 9.5V
HV INTERMITTENT	Instantaneous open at IGSW terminal of HV control ECU
MG2 (NO1) TEMP HIGH	Motor temperature climbed above 174°C (345°F)
MG2 (NO2) TEMP HIGH	Transaxle fluid temperature climbed above 162°C (324°F)
MG2 INV TEMP HIGH	Motor inverter temperature climbed above 111°C (232°F)
MG1 INV TEMP HIGH	Generator inverter temperature climbed above 111°C (232°F)
MAIN BATT LOW	Battery state of charge dropped below 30%

Accessing Active Tests

Some useful HV ECU active tests can be performed by using the diagnostic tester.

Operate the tester, enter Diagnostic Menu and Active Test, and select the Inverter Stop mode. This mode can be used to determine if there is an internal leak in the inverter or the HV control ECU. The test condition is power switch ON (IG), P position, HV system normal, inverter actuation not being disabled, shutting down inverter, and other active tests not being executed. In this mode, keep the inverter power transistor actuation ON.

New Words

abnormality	[,æbnɔː'mæləti]	n. 反常，变态
complaint	[kəm'pleɪnt]	n. 抱怨
conclude	[kən'kluːd]	vt. & vi. 推断（出）
confirm	[kən'fɜːm]	vt. 确认
crank	[kræŋk]	vt. 起动
fail-safe	['feɪlseɪf]	n. & adj. 故障安全（的），失效保护
insufficient	[,ɪnsə'fɪʃnt]	adj. 不足的
interphase	['ɪntəfeɪz]	n. 相间的
malfunction	[,mæl'fʌŋkʃn]	n. 故障，失灵
megger	['megə]	n. 绝缘电阻表
pertain	[pə'teɪn]	vi. 有关，附属，从属

Chapter 6
Trouble Diagnosis and Service of Electric Vehicles

(续)

New Words			
pinpoint	['pɪnpɔɪnt]	vt.	确定
removal	[rɪ'muːvl]	n.	除去，移走
resolver	[rɪ'zɒlvə]	n.	解析器
resort	[rɪ'zɔːt]	n.	应急措施
retrieve	[rɪ'triːv]	vt.	取回，恢复
stress	[stres]	n.	强调，压力，应力
subset	['sʌbset]	n.	子集，子系统
swing	[swɪŋ]	n.	摆动，摆程，振幅
symptom	['sɪmptəm]	n.	症状，征兆

Phrases and Technical Terms	
active test	主动测试
associated with	与……有关的
freeze frame	冻结数据帧
hand-held tester	手持式检测仪
in series	串联
megger tester	绝缘测试仪
motor generator (MG)	电动机/发电机总成
one more time	再一次
open circuit	断路
short circuit	短路，短接
smart key	智能钥匙
stall test	失速试验
wiring harness	线束

NOTES

*1　All electric vehicles and hybrid electric vehicles use high-voltage circuits that if touched with an unprotected hand could cause serious burns or even death.

　　【句子分析】句中，that... or even death 是一个定语从句。

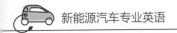

【参考译文】 纯电动汽车和混合动力电动汽车都使用高压电路,如果用无保护的手接触这种高压电路,可能会造成严重烧伤甚至死亡。

*2 Ford requires that a ten-foot insulated fiberglass pole be available outside the safety zone to be used to pull a technician away from the vehicle in the unlikely event of an accident where the technician is shocked or electrocuted.

【句子分析】 that...or electrocuted 是 requires 的宾语从句。在此宾语从句中,where the technician is shocked or electrocuted 是 vehicle 的定语从句。

【参考译文】 福特公司要求,在安全区外应提供一根10ft高的绝缘玻璃钢杆,以便在发生不太可能的意外事故时,将技术人员从他遭受电击即触电的车辆中拉出来。

Chapter 7

Design Aspects of Electric Vehicles
电动汽车设计概略

7.1 Layout of Electric Vehicle Drives
电动汽车传动布置

7.1.1 Layout of Battery Electric Vehicle Drives 纯电动汽车传动布置

Traditional vehicles are modified to add a motor on them instead of IC engine. The original clutch and gear box are retained (Figure 7.1a). In new design, the transmission between the motor and the drive wheels usually has one or two stages of fixed-ratio reduction gear (Figure 7.1b – Figure 7.1e). For most current electric cars, the transmission has a single-stage reduction gear to provide the vehicle with the required hill-climbing capability and the desired maximum speed. In the design as shown Figure7.1d – Figure 7.1f, the differential is eliminated with two motors used. The design as shown in Figure 7.1c is widely used because of its more compact construction, easier installation and simpler control.

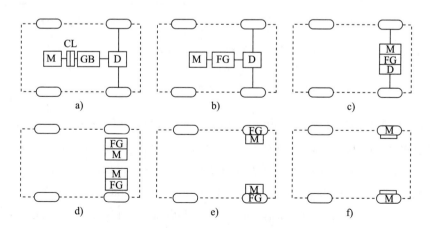

Figure 7.1 Layout of passenger vehicle electric drives

CL—clutch   D—differential   FG—fixed ratio reduction gear   GB—gear box   M—motor

7.1.2 Layout of Hybrid Electric Vehicle Drives
混合动力电动汽车的传动布置

Hybrid drives can be divided into serial hybrid, parallel hybrid and power-split hybrid (also called series-parallel hybrid) drive (Figure 7.2). Serial hybrid is simplest in construction and easiest in control; power-split hybrid is most complicated in construction and control. Nowadays, serial hybrid is mainly used for commercial vehicles and power-split is mainly used for passenger cars.

According to hybridization factor (HF), hybrid drives are current classified into micro hybrid, medium hybrid and full hybrid. Micro and medium hybrids are designed in most cases as parallel hybrids. Full hybrids have been designed as parallel hybrids and power-split hybrids.

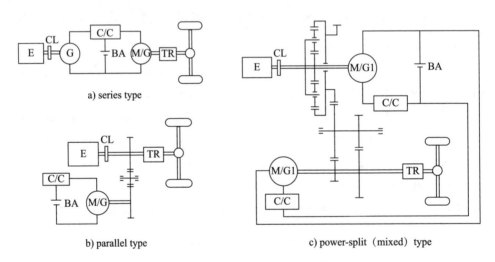

Figure 7.2 Three types of hybrid drives
BA—battery C/C—converter/inverter CL—clutch E—engine
G—generator M/G—motor/generator TR—transmission

The power split hybrid powertrain can fulfill the functions of full hybrid: on board power supply, engine start/stop, electric driving or manoeuvring, boosting and recuperation. The Toyota/Lexus P310 power-split hybrid transmission is an assembly designed specifically for front-transverse hybrid applications and has two high performance electric machines. The structure of this hybrid transmission is shown schematically in Figure 4.15 and Figure 4.16, and its operation is described in Chapter 4.

Chapter 7
Design Aspects of Electric Vehicles

7.1.3 Layout of Commercial Vehicle Serial Hybrid Drives
商用车串联式混合动力驱动布置

Serial hybrid powertrains have a practical relevance for commercial vehicles. They have no mechanical coupling of the engine to the wheels. The serial hybrid drive has the advantage of being highly flexible in terms of the selection of an electrical energy supply source. For all the drive configurations named, the electric traction motors can be arranged as follows:

1) The central motor acting directly on a conventional axle drive; no ratio range. Application: city buses (Figure 7.3a). Possible alternative: design with tandem motors and a summarising gearbox (Figure 7.3c).

2) The central motor acting on a conventional axle drive via a gearbox assembly for speed adjustment, preferably a planetary gearbox; fixed ratio. Application: city buses (Figure 7.3b). Possible alternative: design with tandem motors with two planetary gearboxes and a summarising gearbox (Figure 7.3d).

3) Single-wheel drive with traction motors in direct proximity to the drive wheels (wheel hub drive) as final drive with gearbox assemblies for speed adjustment, preferably planetary gearboxes, often with two-stage design with no ratio range[*1]. Application: city buses, commercial vehicles, special-purpose vehicles (Figure 7.3e).

4) "In-hull drive": single-wheel drive with traction motors, e.g. mounted at the centre of the vehicle, which acts on the drive wheels via propeller shafts. Two-stage selector transmission is possible (shifting when stationary or during operation, with or without power shifting). Application: special wheeled and tracked vehicles (Figure 7.3f).

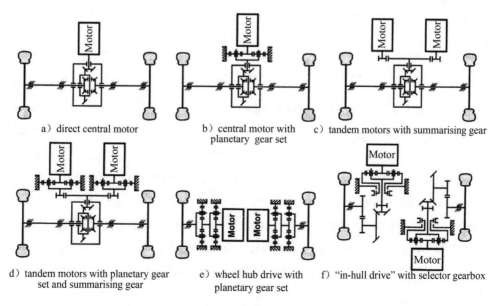

a) direct central motor
b) central motor with planetary gear set
c) tandem motors with summarising gear
d) tandem motors with planetary gear set and summarising gear
e) wheel hub drive with planetary gear set
f) "in-hull drive" with selector gearbox

Figure 7.3 Schematic design types for traction motor applications

New Words

hull	[hʌl]	n. 外壳，船壳，船体
modify	['mɒdɪfaɪ]	vi. 修改，改变，改造
proximity	[prɒk'sɪməti]	n. 接近，邻近
relevance	['reləvəns]	n. 重要性，意义，相关性

Phrases and Technical Terms

drive wheel	驱动车轮，驱动轮
fixed-ratio reduction gear	固定速比减速机构
gear box	齿轮箱
have a relevance for	对……有意义
hill-climbing capability	爬坡能力
in terms of	就……而言
in-hull drive	船体内驱动
planetary gearbox	行星齿轮减速器
power shifting	动力换档
propeller shaft	传动轴
selector transmission	选档式变速器
special wheeled and tracked vehicles	轮式和履带式专用车辆
special-purpose vehicle	专用车辆
summarising gearbox	功率合成齿轮箱
tandem motor	级联电机，双电机
wheel hub drive	轮毂驱动

7.2 Design Criteria of Batteries
蓄电池设计原则

7.2

　　If not designed properly to meet the necessary performance requirements, the battery technology becomes a bottleneck in the early adoption phase of the PEVs. To establish a uniform set of standards for the industry, the United States Advanced Battery Consortium (USABC) has put forth a set of performance objectives for batteries, which are listed in Table 7.1. Based on these objectives, the following critical performance parameters should

Chapter 7
Design Aspects of Electric Vehicles

be carefully considered in PEV applications:

1) *Lifespan* of a battery is an important performance criterion to compete with gas-powered vehicles, as the cost of the batteries is still high. As explained above, there are two primary metrics for measuring the lifespan of batteries, namely cycle life and calendar life. Based on these metrics, the USABC, for instance, aims to have the technology of mass-producing pure electric vehicles of 15-year calendar life and a 1000-cycle life.

Table 7.1 USABC Advance Battery Goals for PEVs in 2020

End of Life Characteristice (30℃)	Unit	Target	Corresponding Vehide Performance
Peak discharge power density, 30s pulse	W/L	1000	Acceleration and size
Peak specific discharge power, 30s pulse	W/kg	470	Acceleration and weight
Usable energy density at $C/3$ discharge rate	W·h/L	500	All-electric-range and size
Usable specific energy at $C/3$ discharge rate	W·h/kg	235	All-electric-range and weight
Usable energy at $C/3$ discharge rate	kW·h	45	All-electric-range, vehicle cost
Calendar life	Years	15	Life-cycle cost
Cycle life	Cycles	1000	Life-cycle cost
Selling price for 100k units	$/kW·h	125	Acquisition cost
Operating environment	℃	−30℃ to 52℃	Battery life
Slow charging time	Hours	<7 with J1772	Battery size cost
Fast charging	Minutes	15 min to 80 SOC	Battery size and cost
Maximum operating voltage	Volts	420	Battery health
Minimum operating voltage	Volts	220	Battery health
Peak current, 30s	Ampere	400	Acceleration
Maximum self-discharge	% per month	<1	All-electric-range

2) *Vehicle performance* should be comparable or superior to that of gas-powered vehicles to gain customer acceptance. PEVs deployed in regions with severe weather conditions (extremely hot or cold) will face additional challenges, as batteries are typically designed to work properly in mild weather conditions. Battery lifetimes are critically sensitive to temperature. Furthermore, solar loading can also lead to further battery heating and reduces battery life. Hence, the USABC is aiming to develop a technology to manufacture batteries that can operate properly in the range of −30℃ to 52℃ without experiencing major degradations.

3) *Specific energy* and power characteristics of the batteries affect various performance

metrics, such as the driving range and weight of the vehicle. Current battery cells have nominal energy densities in the range 140 – 180 W·h/kg, whereas gasoline has the energy density of 13000 W·h/kg. The USABC is aiming to improve the specific energy characteristics from the current levels to 235 W·h/kg. On the other hand, current battery technologies are mature in terms of specific power as PEV batteries can discharge in a short time during acceleration of the vehicle. Therefore, the current specific power levels are marginally sufficient.

4) *Safety* has the utmost significance in PEV batteries, as the vehicles might operate in harsh environmental terrains and conditions, which include exposure to extreme temperatures, severe vibrations, and high rates of charge and discharge. Moreover, Li-ion batteries can ignite if overcharged. The United States National Renewable Energy Laboratory (NREL) specifies the guidelines for battery safety in order to reduce the likelihood of battery failures and remedies to lessen the outcome of incidents such as fires and explosions.

New Words

acceptance	[ək'septəns]	n.	接受，接纳
bottleneck	['bɒtlnek]	n.	瓶颈
comparable	['kɒmpərəbl]	adj.	可比较的，比得上的
consortium	[kən'sɔːtiəm]	n.	财团；组合，共同体
criteria	[kraɪ'tɪərɪə]	n.	标准，准则
guideline	['gaɪdlaɪn]	n.	指导方针，指导原则
harsh	[hɑːʃ]	adj.	严格的，残酷的
lifespan	['laɪfspæn]	n.	寿命
lifetime	['laɪftaɪm]	n.	一生，寿命
likelihood	['laɪklihʊd]	n.	可能，可能性
marginally	['mɑːdʒɪnəli]	adv.	在边缘，在一定程度上，勉强合格
mature	[mə'tʃʊə(r)]	adj.	成熟的
metric	['metrɪk]	n.	度量标准，尺度
remedy	['remədi]	n.	治疗法，补救办法
superior	[suː'pɪəriə(r)]	adj.	较好的，上等的
uniform	['juːnɪfɔːm]	adj.	规格一致的，始终如一的
utmost	['ʌtməʊst]	adj.	极度的，最大的

Chapter 7
Design Aspects of Electric Vehicles

Phrases and Technical Terms	
discharge rate	放电率
have put forth	提出
performance objective	性能目标
performance parameter	性能参数

7.3 Optimization Techniques-Mathematical Modeling
优化技术 – 数学建模

7.3

The effects of design parameters on the performance of an EV can be modeled mathematically. This section presents some of the basic techniques. Refer to Figure 7.4 and Table 7.2 for an explanation of the symbols.

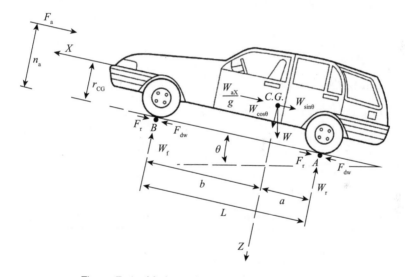

Figure 7.4 Mathematical modeling-values used

Table 7.2 Explanation of the symbols

F_a	Aerodynamic drag force
ρ	Density of air
C_d	Coefficient of drag, e.g. 0.3 to 0.4
A_f	Area of the vehicle front
V_v	Velocity of the vehicle
V_{wind}	Velocity of the wind
F_r	Rolling resistive force

105

（续）

μ_r	Road coefficient of friction	
μ_{const}	Tyre rolling coefficient of friction	
F_c	Climbing resistive force	
m	Mass of the vehicle (total)	
g	Acceleration due to gravity	
θ	Angle of the hill	
$F_{resistive}$	Total resistive force	
F_{dw}	Force developed at the driving wheels	
η_e	Efficiency of the electric motor	
η_m	Efficiency of the mechanical transmission	
a	Centre of gravity position within the wheel base	
μ_a	Coefficient of road adhesion	
W	Weight of the vehicle (mg)	
L	Length of the wheel base	
h_{cg}	Height of the vehicle's centre of gravity	
J_{eff}	Total effective inertia of the vehicle	
M_B	Mass of the battery	
Y	Power density of the battery	
X_i	Correlation between energy density as a function of power density	

Aerodynamic drag force

$$F_a = \frac{\rho C_d A_f}{2} (V_v \pm V_{wind})^2$$

Rolling resistive force

$$F_r = \mu_r mg \cos\theta$$

Climbing resistive force

$$F_c = mg \sin\theta$$

Therefore the total resistive force is

$$F_{resistive} = F_a + F_r + F_c$$

Chapter 7
Design Aspects of Electric Vehicles

Force developed at the wheels

$$F_{dw} = F_{motor} \eta_e \eta_m$$

The tractive effort therefore is

$$F_{tractive} = F_{dw} - F_{resistive}$$

The maximum tractive force that can be developed

$$F_{dwmax} = \frac{\alpha \mu_a W/L}{1 + \mu_a h_{cg}/L}$$

The effective mass of a vehicle is

$$m_{eff} = m + \frac{J_{eff}}{r^2}$$

Acceleration time can now be shown to be

$$t = m_{eff} \int_{V_1}^{V_2} \frac{dV}{F_{tractive}}$$

Power required to hold the vehicle at a constant speed

$$Power = \frac{V_v F_{resistive}}{\eta_e \eta_m}$$

Power density of the batteries

$$y = \frac{Power}{M_s}$$

The correlation between energy density as a function of power density can be calculated

$$x_i = ay^5 + by^4 + cy^3 + dy^2 + ey + f$$

The range of the vehicle from fully charged batteries can be calculated from

$$Hours = \frac{x_i}{y}$$

$$Range = V_v \, Hours$$

Further calculations are possible to allow modeling a subject which, if grasped, can save an enormous amount of time and money during development.

New Words

aerodynamic	[ˌeərəʊdaɪˈnæmɪk]	adj. 空气动力（学）的
explanation	[ˌekspləˈneɪʃn]	n. 解释，说明
mathematically	[ˌmæθəˈmætɪklɪ]	adv. 数学上地
model	[ˈmɒdl]	vt. 制作模型，模仿，模拟
technique	[tekˈniːk]	n. 技巧，技能，技术

Phrases and Technical Terms

acceleration time	加速时间
aerodynamic drag force	空气阻力
climbing resistive force	爬坡阻力
design parameter	设计参数
effect of ... on ...	……对……的影响
rolling resistive force	滚动阻力
total resistive force	总阻力
tractive effort	驱动力

NOTES

*1 Single-wheel drive with traction motors in direct proximity to the drive wheels (wheel hub drive) as final drive with gearbox assemblies for speed adjustment, preferably planetary gearboxes, often with two-stage design with no ratio range.

【句子分析】这是名词短语。Single-wheel drive 后面跟着两个长长的介词短语。第一个介词短语是 with traction motors in direct proximity to the drive wheels (wheel hub drive)，第二个介词短语是 as final drive with gearbox assemblies for speed adjustment, preferably planetary gearboxes, often with two-stage design with no ratio range，这两个介词短语均为 single-wheel drive 的后置定语。

第一个介词短语的结构是介词 with 后面为名词+介词（或分词）+名词的结构，在逻辑上这是"主谓宾"结构。

第二个介词短语 as final drive... 中还有三个 with 介词短语。第一个 with 介词短语（with gearbox assemblies for speed adjustment, preferably planetary gearboxes）在 with 后面也有逻辑上的"主谓宾"关系；第二个 with 介词短语（often with two-stage design）作为 gearbox assemblies 的后置定语；第三个 with 介词短语（with no ratio range）作为 two-stage design 的后置定语。

【参考译文】牵引电机紧靠驱动轮（轮毂驱动）的单轮驱动装置，作为最终传动它采用变速器组件以便于速度调整，变速器组件最好是行星齿轮变速器，通常是两级设计，且没有速比变化范围。

*2 The United States National Renewable Energy Laboratory (NREL) specifies the guidelines for battery safety in order to reduce the likelihood of battery failures and remedies to lessen the outcome of incidents such as fires and explosions.

【句子分析】 guidelines for battery safety 与 remedies 并列为 specifies 的宾语。这两个宾语后面各有一个动词不定式充当后置定语。

【参考译文】 美国国家可再生能源实验室（NREL）规定了旨在降低电池故障的可能性的电池安全准则和旨在减轻火灾和爆炸等事件造成的后果的补救措施。

Chapter 8

Fuel Cell Powered Vehicles
燃料电池汽车

8.1 Overview of Fuel Cell technology
燃料电池技术概述

A fuel cell is a device that directly converts the chemical energy of a fuel into electrical energy, in the form of low-voltage direct current electricity. The most common fuel used in the fuel cell is hydrogen (H_2). Fuel cells that convert the chemical energy of methanol (CH_3OH) directly into electrical energy have also been developed. The oxidant for the fuel cell is usually atmospheric oxygen (O_2).

8.1.1 Classification of Fuel Cell 燃料电池分类

Many types of fuel cell are available, such as proton exchange membrane (polymer electrolyte membrane) fuel cell, solid oxide fuel cell, phosphoric acid fuel cell, alkaline fuel cell, and molten carbonate fuel cell. For vehicle applications, the proton exchange membrane fuel cell (PEMFC) is considered to be the most promising. This is because it has high power density, long life, and low corrosion, and operates in a reasonable temperature range (80℃ - 100℃).

8.1.2 Construction and Operation of Fuel Cell 燃料电池的结构与运行

Construction of Fuel Cell

A schematic diagram of a proton exchange membrane fuel cell (PEMFC) is shown in Figure 8.1. A PEMFC consists of the following basic components:
- Electrodes. There are a fuel electrode (anode) and an oxidant electrode (cathode). They are made of porous, electrically and thermally conducting material, such as porous graphite. The anode and cathode are connected with an external electric

circuit through bipolar plates.
- Electrolyte. The PEMFC uses proton exchange membrane as the electrolyte. The requirements for the membrane are high proton conductivity, high chemical and thermal stability, good durability, and low cost. The membrane currently in wide use is made of perfluorosulfonate（全氟磺酸盐）material.

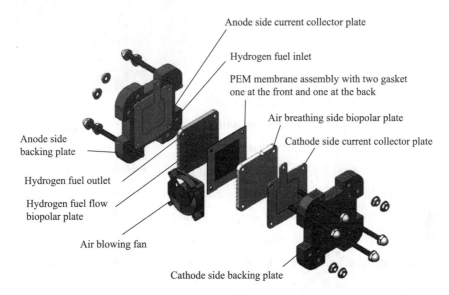

Figure 8.1 A schematic diagram of a proton exchange membrane fuel cell

- Catalyst Layers. There is one catalyst layer on either side of the membrane. It is on the catalyst surface where the electrochemical reactions take place[*1]. The most commonly used catalyst is platinum or platinum alloy. The anode, cathode, membrane, and two catalyst layers are usually sealed together to form a single membrane electrode assembly (MEA).
- Gas Diffusion Layers. This arrangement consists of one gas diffusion layer in contact with the anode and one with the cathode. Their functions are to ensure that the hydrogen gas or air diffuses evenly and efficiently over the catalyst layer, to provide uniform distribution of load on the surface of the MEA from the bipolar plate and to provide electrical conduction between the bipolar plate and the anode or cathode[*2]. It is made of porous carbon paper or cloth treated with polytetrafluoroethylene.
- Bipolar Plates. These are commonly made of graphite or conducting metal (such as coated titanium). Gas flow channels are machined into the plates to provide inlets for the hydrogen gas and air, as well as outlets for excess hydrogen gas for recirculation and for water produced in the fuel cell.

These elements above mentioned form an individual cell. A fuel-cell stack is made up of hundreds of individual cells connected in series. The fuel cells are placed end to end in the stack, much like slices in a loaf of bread, as shown in Figure 8.2. Automotive fuel-cell stacks contain more than 400 cells in their construction.

Figure 8.2　A fuel-cell stack

Operation of Fuel Cell

In operation, hydrogen gas is fed to the fuel cell. It diffuses through the gas diffusion layer and the anode and comes into contact with the catalyst surface. On the catalyst surface, electrochemical reactions take place. The hydrogen is split into electrons (e^-) and hydrogen protons (H^+). The flow of electrons from the anode to the cathode, and through the bipolar plates, forms electric current, which is used to drive an external load, such as an electric motor or a bulb. The hydrogen protons pass through the proton exchange membrane and interact with the electrons and oxygen in an electrochemical process at the catalyst surface on the cathode side, as shown in Figure 8.3.

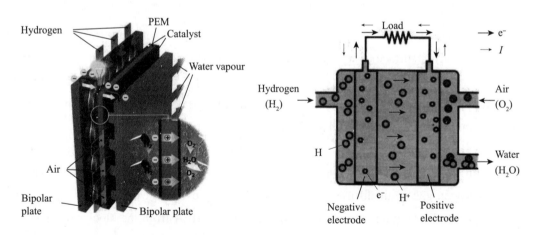

Figure 8.3　Operation principle of fuel cell

Anode (negative electrode) reaction

$$H_2 \rightarrow 2H^+ + 2e^-$$

Cathode (positive electrode) reaction

$$2H^+ + 2e^- + 1/2O_2 \rightarrow H_2O$$

Total reaction

$$H_2 + 1/2 O_2 \rightarrow H_2O$$

As a result of electrochemical reactions, water and heat are produced. Consequently, water and thermal management is one of the issues that require careful consideration in the design of the fuel cell. The precise control of the flow and pressure of hydrogen gas and air and of temperature and membrane humidity is critical to the efficient operation of the fuel cell.

8.1.3 Water and Heat Management of Fuel Cell 燃料电池的水和热管理

Water management inside a PEM fuel cell is critical. Too much water can prevent oxygen from making contact with the positive electrode; too little water can allow the electrolyte to dry out and lower its conductivity. The role of the humidifier is to achieve a balance where it is providing sufficient moisture to the fuel cell by recycling water that is evaporating at the cathode. The humidifier is located in the air line leading to the cathode of the fuel-cell stack.

Heat is generated by the fuel cell during normal operation. Excess heat can lead to a breakdown of the polymer electrolyte membrane, so a liquid cooling system must be utilized to remove waste heat from the fuel-cell stack.

In a Honda FCX fuel cell vehicle, the humidifier and fuel cell radiator are shown in Figure 8.4.

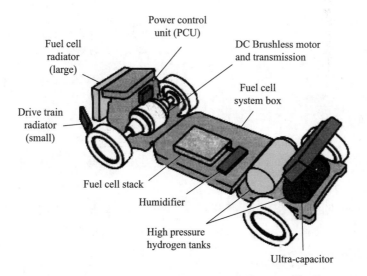

Figure 8.4 Power train layout in a Honda FCX fuel cell vehicle

New Words

alloy	[ˈælɔɪ]	n.	合金
anode	[ˈænəʊd]	n.	阳极
atmospheric	[ˌætməsˈferɪk]	adj.	大气的
carbonate	[ˈkɑːbəneɪt]	n.	碳酸盐
conductivity	[ˌkɒndʌkˈtɪvəti]	n.	传导性，导电性
corrosion	[kəˈrəʊʒn]	n.	腐蚀，侵蚀
diagram	[ˈdaɪəɡræm]	n.	图表，图解，示意图
diffuse	[dɪˈfjuːs]	vi.	传播，分散
durability	[ˌdjʊərəˈbɪləti]	n.	耐久性，持久性
humidifier	[hjuːˈmɪdɪfaɪə(r)]	n.	增湿器，加湿器
humidity	[hjuːˈmɪdəti]	n.	湿度
oxidant	[ˈɒksɪdənt]	n.	氧化剂
phosphoric	[fɒsˈfɒrɪk]	adj.	磷的，含磷的
platinum	[ˈplætɪnəm]	n.	铂，白金
porous	[ˈpɔːrəs]	adj.	能穿透的，多孔性的
promising	[ˈprɒmɪsɪŋ]	adj.	有前途的，有希望的

Phrases and Technical Terms

air line	空气管路
alkaline fuel cell	碱性燃料电池
bipolar plate	双极板
carbon paper	碳纸，复写纸
dry out	变干
fuel-cell stack	燃料电池堆
in contact with	与……接触
in the form of	以……形式
individual cell	单体电池
membrane electrode assembly (MEA)	膜电极
molten carbonate fuel cell	熔融碳酸盐燃料电池
phosphoric acid fuel cell	磷酸燃料电池
proton exchange membrane	质子交换膜
proton exchange membrane fuel cell (PEMFC)	质子交换膜燃料电池
solid oxide fuel cell	固体氧化物燃料电池

Chapter 8
Fuel Cell Powered Vehicles

8.2 Fuel Cell Electric Vehicle (FCEV) and Fuel Cell Hybrid Electric Vehicle (FCHEV)
燃料电池电动汽车 (FCEV) 与燃料电池混合动力汽车 (FCHEV)

8.2.1 Components and Layout of FCEV and FCHEV
FCEV 与 FCHEV 的部件及布置

A fuel cell electric vehicle consists of fuel tank (hydrogen tank or methanol tank), fuel cell stack, power control unit (converter and inverter) and traction motor (Figure 1.7). On a FCEV, hydrogen may be either stored onboard or derived from another fuel, such as gasoline or other hydrocarbon fuels, using an onboard chemical reforming system.

Fuel cell hybrid electric vehicle (FCHEV) depends on another energy storage system (ESS) for supporting the fuel cell. Depending on the power demand and supply a battery or ultra-capacitor can be used as the ESS which can be charged or discharged. An example of an FCHEV power train is shown in Figure 8.4. With respect to fuel, hydrogen is widely used in the fuel cell electric vehicles and fuel cell hybrid electric vehicles now developed and demonstrated (Table 8.1).

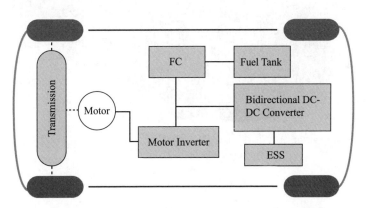

Figure 8.5 Power train layout of fuel cell hybrid vehicle

Table 8.1 Some recent developed fuel cell vehicles

Vehicle model	Type	Energy source	Fuel economy MPGe (City/highway)	Range/mile
Honda Clarity fuel cell 2017	FCHEV	Hydrogen	–	434
Toyota Mirai 2016	FCEV	Hydrogen	66/66	312
Audi Sportback	FCHEV	Hydrogen	39/43	400 – 500

(续)

Vehicle model	Type	Energy source	Fuel economy MPGe (City/highway)	Range/mile
Kia Borrego FCEV	FCEV	Hydrogen	–	426
Hyundai ix35 2013	FCEV	Hydrogen	49/51	265
Mercedes-Benz F800 2010	FCEV	Hydrogen	–	435

8.2.2 GM HydroGen4 Fuel Cell Electric Vehicle
通用 HydroGen4 燃料电池电动汽车

Since autumn 2007, more than 100 cars of the HydroGen4 shown in Figure 8.5 were demonstrated in countries like Germany and the United states. From Table 8.2, it is seen that the GM HydroGen4 could offer a higher performance than other EVs. The car could be operated and started very low temperature down to -25℃.

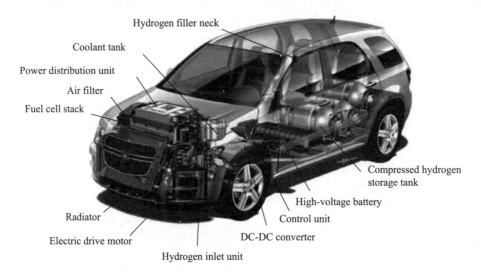

Figure 8.6 GM HydroGen4 fuel cell electric vehicle

From the technical data (Table 8.2), the electrical propulsion provides excellent performance for the vehicle. Three carbon-fiber tanks on-board store 4.2 kg of hydrogen and enable a range of 320 km. The empty hydrogen storage system can be completely refilled within 3 min. A nickel metal-hydride battery (Ni-MH) with an energy content of 1.8 kW·h is also installed on-board to improve the agility of the vehicle and also to increase the efficiency.

Chapter 8
Fuel Cell Powered Vehicles

Table 8.2 Specifications of the GM HydroGen4 fuel cell electric vehicle

Vehicle type		Five-door, crossover vehicle, front-wheel drive
Dimensions, Weight and Payload	Length	4796 mm
	Width	1814 mm
	Height	1760 mm
	Wheelbase	2858 mm
	Trunk space	906 L
	Weight	2010 kg
	Payload	340 kg
Hydrogen storage system	Type	3 Type IV CGH2 Vessels
	Operating pressure	70 MPa
Fuel cell system	Type	PEM
	Cells	440
	Power	93 kW
Battery system	Type	Ni-MH
	Power	35 kW
	Capacity	1.8 kW·h
Electric propulsion system	Type	Three-phase, synchronous motor
	Maximum power	94 kW
	Maximum torque	320N·m
Performance	Top speed	160 km/h
	Acceleration (0-100 km/h)	12s
	Range	320 km
	Operating temperature	25-45℃

New Words		
agility	[əˈdʒɪləti]	n. 敏捷，活泼，灵活
derive	[dɪˈraɪv]	vt.&vi. 源于，来自
ultra-capacitor	[ˈʌltrə kəˈpæsɪtə(r)]	n. 超级电容器

Phrases and Technical Terms	
chemical reforming	化学重整
energy storage system (ESS)	储能系统

*1 It is on the catalyst surface where the electrochemical reactions take place.

【句子分析】这是一个强调句，强调做状语的介词短语 on the catalyst surface。

【参考译文】就是在催化剂表面上发生着电化学反应。

*2 Their functions are to ensure that the hydrogen gas or air diffuses evenly and efficiently over the catalyst layer, to provide uniform distribution of load on the surface of the MEA from the bipolar plate and to provide electrical conduction between the bipolar plate and the anode or cathode.

【句子分析】动词不定式 to ensure 后面跟着一个宾语从句。从语法上看，宾语从句可以从 that 开始一直到句末，且认为两个 to provide … 动词不定式短语是并列关系，是从句的结果状语。这样得到的译文为"它们（气体扩散层）的功能是确保氢气或空气在催化剂层上均匀有效地扩散，从而提供来自双极板的作用于 MEA 表面上的均布载荷，并在双极板与阳极或阴极之间提供导电功能。"仔细看这段译文，显然前后意思是不通的（提供均布载荷和提供导电功能怎么能是气体均匀扩散的结果呢？），因此上述划分一定是错误的。

再看主语 functions 为复数形式，即说明本句介绍了多个功能，那么句中三个动词不定式（或至少两个）可能为并列的表语，说明不同的功能。再尝试着从语意上进行判断，三个动词不定式的确为并列关系，说明三个不同的功能。

由此看出，语法分析与含义的逻辑描述均正确，译文才能正确。

【参考译文】它们（气体扩散层）的作用有三个：确保氢气或空气在催化剂层上均匀有效地扩散，提供来自双极板的作用于 MEA 表面上的均布载荷（夹持力），并在双极板与阳极或阴极之间提供导电功能。

Chapter 9

CNG-Gasoline Dual-fuel Vehicles
压缩天然气-汽油双燃料汽车

9.1 Natural Gas Nature and Features
天然气的性质与特点

9.1

Natural gas is a fossil fuel consisting primarily of methane (CH_4). The percentage of actual methane contained in natural gas runs at 80% to 99%, depending on the region where the gas is extracted. The rest is made up of carbon dioxide, nitrogen and low-grade hydrocarbons. Natural gas can be stored in a vehicle either in liquid form at -162℃ as LNG (liquefied natural gas) or in compressed form at pressures of up to 200 bar as CNG (compressed natural gas)[*1]. Natural gas is generally used in its compressed form because of the high cost of storing the liquefied version.

The high knock resistance of natural gas (approx. 140 RON) allows a compression of roughly 13:1. However, this advantage cannot be exploited in bivalent drives, i.e. in a combination of petrol and natural-gas drives, because the compression ratio must be tuned to petrol operation.

Advantages of natural-gas drive over spark-ignition and diesel engines:
- Very good combustion properties and low emissions of CO_2, NO_x, CO and virtually no particulate and sulphur emissions.
- Less carbon fouling of spark plugs and reduced contamination of engine oil.

Disadvantages of natural-gas drive in comparison with spark-ignition and diesel engines:
- Lower engine power due to the lower calorific value of natural gas.
- Expensive storage of natural gas necessary.
- Shorter cruising range with the same tank volume.

- Extensive safety regulations with regard to operating, servicing and repairing natural-gas vehicles.

New Words

approx.	[əˈprɒks]	adv. 大约（= approximately）
bivalent	[baɪˈveɪlənt]	adj. 二价的；n. 二价体
comparison	[kəmˈpærɪsn]	n. 比较，对照
contamination	[kənˌtæmɪˈneɪʃən]	n. 污染
fossil	[ˈfɒsl]	adj. 化石的，陈腐的
fouling	[ˈfaʊlɪŋ]	n. 污垢
nitrogen	[ˈnaɪtrədʒən]	n. 氮
particulate	[pɑːˈtɪkjələt]	n. 微粒
roughly	[ˈrʌfli]	adv. 粗略地，大体上
sulphur	[ˈsʌlfə(r)]	n. 硫磺

Phrases and Technical Terms

bivalent drive	双元驱动
calorific value	热值
carbon dioxide	二氧化碳
combustion property	燃烧特性
fossil fuel	化石燃料，矿物燃料
in comparison with	与……相比
knock resistance	抗爆性
liquefied natural gas	液化天然气
with regard to	关于……，就……

9.2 Construction of CNG-Gasoline Dual-fuel Vehicle
CNG-汽油双燃料汽车的构造

Natural-gas drives are generally used in combination with petrol operation in spark-ignition engines (so-called bivalent drives). Various additional components must be installed in the vehicle for this purpose (Figure 9.1).

Chapter 9
CNG-Gasoline Dual-fuel Vehicles

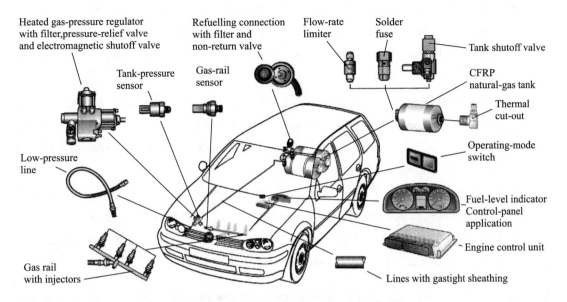

Figure 9.1 Layout of a CNG vehicle

Operating Principle

The natural gas stored at approx. 200 bars in the natural-gas tank flows to the gas-pressure regulator. This regulates the gas pressure in several reducing stages at approx. 9 bars. The gas injectors in the intake manifold are energised by the ECU as required and thereby opened[*2]. The gas mixes with the inducted air and then flows as a gas-air mixture into the combustion chamber.

Safety Features

Natural-gas drives pose certain risks to the environment, e.g. as a result of the unchecked discharge of gas or the danger of explosion caused by a rise in pressure. For this reason, these systems are equipped with various safety features.

- Non-return valves. These are located in the refuelling connection and on the tank shut off valves and prevent the gas from flowing back via the refuelling valve.
- Gastight sheathing. This is wrapped round the lines and components routed inside the vehicle.
- Screwed joints. These are designed as double clamping-ring screwed connections.
- Natural-gas tanks. These are made of steel or CFRP. Each tank is connected by two retainers to the vehicle. The burst pressures are approx. 400 bars for steel tanks and approx. 500 bars for CFRP tanks.

- Solder fuse and thermal cut-out on the natural gas tank. These prevent an excessive pressure increase and thus the tank from exploding in the event of a fire.
- Flow-rate limiter. This prevents the natural-gas tank from draining suddenly in the event of a pipe breakage.
- Electromagnetic shutoff valves. This valve, which is mounted on the natural-gas tank, closes on changeover to petrol mode, in the event of a power failure, when the engine is stopped or in the event of an accident. A further shutoff valve is located on the pressure regulator.
- Flexible gas lines. These prevent breaks caused by fatigue failure on the low-pressure side, i.e. between the pressure regulator and the gas injectors.
- Overpressure regulator. This is mounted on the pressure regulator and protects the low-pressure side against excessive pressures.

New Words

fatigue	[fə'tiːg]	n. 疲劳，疲乏
gastight	['gæstaɪt]	adj. 不漏气的，气密
retainer	[rɪ'teɪnə(r)]	n. 护圈，隔环
route	[ruːt]	vt. 通路选定，迂回
sheath	[ʃiːθ]	n. 护套；vt. 包

Phrases and Technical Terms

gas-pressure regulator	气压调节器
gas injector	气体喷射器
combustion chamber	燃烧室
shut off valve	截止阀
refuelling valve	充气阀
clamping-ring	夹紧环，卡箍
CFRP	碳纤维增强塑料
burst pressure	爆裂压力
solder fuse	焊料熔断器
thermal cut-out	热熔熔断器
low-rate limiter	流量限制器
fatigue failure	疲劳失效
overpressure regulator	过电压调节器

9.3 Service Notes
维护提示

If the high-pressure gas tank is replaced at regular intervals and the system is subjected to a service-inspection in accordance with the manufacturer's instructions, then there is no need to subject the gas system to the prescribed recurring checks.

The following components of the natural-gas system must be checked within the framework of a service-inspection:
- Natural-gas tanks and lines.
- Electromagnetic shutoff valves.
- Closing cap and natural-gas filler neck.
- Vent lines on the natural-gas tanks.

Leak tests must be carried out in accordance with the manufacturer's instructions, e. g. with a gas-leak detector.

New Words		
instruction	[ɪnˈstrʌkʃn]	n. 规程，说明（书）
prescribed	[prɪˈskraɪbd]	adj. 规定的

Phrases and Technical Terms	
gas-leak detector	气体泄漏检测器，检漏仪
recurring check	反复检查
subject... to ...	使……经受……

NOTES

*1 Natural gas can be stored in a vehicle either in liquid form at -162℃ as LNG (liquefied natural gas) or in compressed form at pressures of up to 200 bar as CNG (compressed natural gas).
【句子分析】介词短语 in liquid form ... 与 in compressed form ... 并列。
【参考译文】在车辆上，天然气可以在-162℃以液态形式作为 LNG（液化天然气）储存，或在压力高达 200 巴以压缩的形式作为 CNG（压缩天然气）储存。

*2 The gas injectors in the intake manifold are energised by the ECU as required and thereby opened.
【句子分析】句末 opened 与 energised 并列。
【参考译文】进气歧管中的气体喷射器在 ECU 控制下按要求通电，从而开启。

附 录

附录A 丰田普锐斯混合动力控制系统故障诊断数据

A.1 丰田普锐斯混合动力控制系统故障码信息（Table A.1）

Table A.1 Toyota Prius Hybrid control system DTC Information

Hand-held Tester Display	Measurement Item/Range (Display)	Suspected Vehicle Status When Malfunction Occurs
INFORMATION N	Information code	Indication of system with malfunction
MG1 REV	MG1 revolution/ Min.: −16384 rpm, Max.: 16256 rpm	MG1 speed • Forward rotation appears as " + " • Backward rotation appears as " − "
MG2 REV	MG2 revolution/ Min.: −16384 rpm, Max.: 16256 rpm	MG2 speed (proportionate to vehicle speed) • Forward rotation appears as " + " • Backward rotation appears as " − " Moving direction of vehicle • Forward direction appears as " + " • Backward direction appears as " − "
MG1 TORQ	MG1 torque/ Min.: −512 N·m, Max.: 508 N·m	When MG1 rotation in + direction: • Torque appears as " + " while MG1 discharges • Torque appears as " − " while MG1 charges When MG1 rotation in − direction: • Torque appears as " − " while MG1 discharges • Torque appears as " + " while MG1 charges

(续)

Hand-held Tester Display	Measurement Item/Range (Display)	Suspected Vehicle Status When Malfunction Occurs
MG2 TORQ	MG2 torgue/ Min.: −512 N·m, Max.: 508 N·m	When MG2 rotation in + direction; • Torque appears as " + " while MG2 discharges • Torque appears as " − " while MG2 charges When MG2 rotation in − direction; • Torque appears as " − " while MG2 discharges • Torque appears as " + " while MG2 charges
INVERT TEMP – MG1	MG1 inverter temperature/ Min.: −50℃, Max.: 205℃	MG1 inverter temperature
INVERT TEMP – MG2	MG2 inverter temperature/ Min.: −50℃, Max.: 205℃	MG2 inverter temperature
MG2 TEMP (No2)	Transaxle fluid temperature/ Min.: −50℃, Max.: 205℃	Transaxle fluid temperature
MG2 TEMP (No1)	MG2 temperature/ Min.: −50℃, Max.: 205℃	MG2 temperature
POWER RQST	Request engine power/ Min.: 0 W, Max.: 255 kW	Engine power output requested to ECM
MCYL CTRL POWER	Master cylinder control torque/ Min.: 512 N·m, Max.: 508 N·m	Engine speed
SOC	Battery state of charge/ Min.: 0%, Max.: 100%	State of charge of HV battery
WOUT CTRL POWER	Power value discharge control/ Min.: 0 W, Max.: 81600 W	Discharge amount of HV battery

(续)

Hand-held Tester Display	Measurement Item/Range (Display)	Suspected Vehicle Status When Malfunction Occurs
WIN CTRL POWER	Power value charge control/ Min.: -40800 W, Max.: 0 W	Charge amount of HV battery
DRIVE CONDITION	Drive condition ID • Engine stopped: 0 • Engine about to be stopped: 1 • Engine about to be started: 2 • Engine operated or operating: • Generating or loading movement: • Revving up with P position: 6	Engine operating condition
PWR RESOURCE VB	HV battery voltage/ Min.: 0 V, Max.: 510V	HV battery voltage
PWR RESOURCE IB	HV battery current/ Min.: -256 A, Max.: 254 A	Charging/discharging state of HV battery • Discharging amperage indicated by a positive value • Charging amperage indicated by a negative value
SHIFT POSITION	Shift position (P, R, N, D or B position)	Shift position
ACCEL SENSOR MAIN	Accelerator pedal position sensor main/ Min.: 0%, Max.: 100%	Idling, accelerating, or decelerating
AUX. BATT V	Auxiliary battery voltage/ Min.: 0 V, Max.: 20V	State of aupdiliary battery
CONVERTER TEMP	Boost converter temperature/ Min.: -50℃, Max.: 205℃	Boost converter temperature
VL	High voltage before it is boosted/ Min.: 0 V, Max.: 510V	High voltage level before it is boosted

(续)

Hand-held Tester Display	Measurement Item/Range (Display)	Suspected Vehicle Status When Malfunction Occurs
VH	High voltage after it is boosted/ Min. : 0 V, Max. : 765V	High voltage level after it is boosted
IG ON TIME	The time after power switch ON (IG) / Min. : 0 min, Max. : 255 min	Time elapsed with power switch ON (IG)
VEHICLE SPD – MAX	Maximum vehicle speed/ Min. : −256 km/h, Max. : 254 km/h	Maximum vehicle speed
A/C CONSMPT PWR	A/C consumption power/ Min: 0 kW, Max. : 5 kW	A/C load
ENG STOP RQST	Engine stop request/ NO or YES	Presence of engine stop request
IDLING REQUEST	Engine idling request/ NO or YES	Presence of idle stop request
ENGINE FUEL CUT	Engine fuel cut request/ NO or YES	Presence of fuel cut request
HV BATT CH RQST	HV battery charging request/ NO or YES	Presence of HV battery charging request
ENG WARM UP RQT	Engine warming up request/ NO or YES	Presence of engine warm – up request
STOP SW COND	Stop lamp switch ON condition/ NO or YES	Brake pedal depressed or released
CRUISE CONTROL	Cruise control active condition/ NO or YES	Operation under cruise control ON or OFF
EXCLUSIVE INFO 1 to 7	Exclusive information (in form of numerical data)	Exclusive Information linked to Information
OCCURRENCE ORDER	Occurrence sequence of information	Occurrence sequence of information
INV TTMP – MG1 IG	MG1 inverter temperature after power switch ON (IG) / Min. : −50°C, Max. : 205°C	MG1 inverter temperature soon after power switch ON (IG)
INVT TMP – MG2 IG	MG2 inverter temperature after power switch ON (IG) / Min. : −50°C, Max. : 205°C	MG2 inverter temperature soon after power switch ON (IG)

(续)

Hand-held Tester Display	Measurement Item/Range (Display)	Suspected Vehicle Status When Malfunction Occurs
MG2 TEMP IG	MG2 temperature after power switch ON (IG) / Min.: -50℃, Max.: 205℃	MG2 temperature soon after power switch ON (IG)
CONVRTR TEMP IG	Boost converter temperature after power switch ON (IG) / Min. -50°C, Max.: 205℃ (IG)	Boost converter temperature soon after power switch ON (IG)
SOC IG	Battery state of charge after power switch ON (IG) / Min.: 0 %, Max.: 100 %	Battery state of charge soon after power switch ON (IG)
INVT TMP - MG1 MAX	MG1 inverter maximum temperature/ Min.: -50°C, Max.: 205℃	Overheating state of MG1 inverter
INVT TMP - MG2 MAX	MG2 inverter maximum temperature/ Min.: -50℃, Max.: 205℃	Overheating state of MG2 inverter
MG2 TEMP MAX	MG2 maximum temperature/ Min.: -50℃, Max.: 205℃	Overheating state of MG2
CONVRTR TMP MAX	Boost converter maximum temperature/ Min.: -50℃, Max.: 205℃	Overheating state of boost converter
SOC MAX	Maximum status of charge/Min.: 0 %, Max.: 100 %	Over-charging of HV battery
SOC MIN	Minimum status of charge/Min.: 0 %, Max.: 100 %	Over-discharging of HV battery

A.2 丰田普锐斯混合动力控制系统操作历史数据（Table A.2）

Table A.2 Toyota Prius Hybrid Control System Operation History Data

Items	Count Condition	Example of Customer Concern	Actual Status
SHIFT BEF READY	The number of times of shift operation while the Ready lamp is flashing (just after turning to ST). Flashes if cooling water temp. is −10℃ or less. Illuminates if cooling water temperature is above −10℃	Engine starts and immediately stops in the morning. Couldn't drive the vehicle	Engine was in cranking condition and Ready lamp was flashing, however, the costumer judged the engine is running from the generator noise by mistake
N RANGE CTRL 2	The number of times of shifting from R to D. (Shift into R range when driving D range or vice versa)	Shifting into R range, but vehicle went ahead	Shift lever was in N range while going ahead at 11km/h
STEP ACCEL IN N	The number times of stepping on the accelerator pedal in N range. No driving force is supplide due to shift in N range condition at accelerator operation	Sometimes power isn't generated when driving	Stepping on the accelerator when in the N range. Because it is under N range control, torque is not generated
AUX. BATTLOW	The number of times of N range control when voltage of the 12V auxiliary battery falls to 9.5V or less	Acceleration didn't work suddenly	
HV INTERMITTENT	Instantaneous open at IGSW terminal of HV control ECU	Suddenly the vehicle stopped, but ran as usual after operating key again	If HV ECU power supply line was disconnected, system itself stopped and power supply was shut down before fixing abnormal occurrence. Consequently, the DTC was not stored and it is impossible to judge what occurred. From this experience, system was modified so as to record momentary shutting down

(续)

Items	Count Condition	Example of Customer Concern	Actual Status
MG2 (NO1) TEMP HIGH	The number of times the water temperature warning lamp is ON due to MG2 temperature rise Lamp illuminates if motor temperature rises above 174℃ (345°F) DTC is not stored because it is not a problem even if warning lamp in ON	Warning Lamp ON	Specification if motor/generator/inverter temperature rises to illuminate turtle lamp (2001-2003 Prius). It is difficult to identify what caused lamp illumination. From this experience, it is modified to recored the number of times of symptoms occurence by parts. It is also modified to assign a role of warning of such temperature rise to water temperature indicator
MG2 (NO2) TEMP HIGH	The number of times the water temperature waning lamp turns ON due to MG1 temperature rise Lamp illuminates transaxle fluid temperature rises above 162℃ (324°F) DTC is not stored because it is not a problem even if warning lamp in ON	Warning Lamp turns on	
MG2 INV TEMP HIGH	Motor inverter temperature rose above 111℃ (232°F)		Specification if motor/generator/inverter temperature rises to illuminate turtle lamp. It is difficult to identify what caused lamp illumination. From this experience, it is modified to record the number of times of symptoms occurrence by parts. It is also modified to assign a role of warning of such temperature rise to water temperature indicator
MG1 INV TEMP HIGH	The number of times the water temp warning lamp turns ON due to MG2 temperature sensor rise in the inverter Lamp illuminates if MG2 temperature rises above 111℃ (232°F) without storing any DTCs because of the problem	Warning Lamp turns on	

(续)

Items	Count Condition	Example of Customer Concern	Actual Status
MAIN BATT LOW	Battery temperature rises to 57℃ and over or falls to −15℃ less. SOC becomes 35% or less in R range and WOUT is controlled to be 2000W	Loss of power momentarily (Turtle light turns ON 2001 - 2003 Prius)	Battery output/input is controlled when battery temperature is abnormal and SOC is Lo. But as it is not a problem, indicate no DTC
RESIST OVR HEAT	The number of times of heating up the resistance for SMR1 Limit resistor forecast temperature rose above 120℃ (248°F)	Vehicle will not start	Prohibits system starting to prevent from overheating SMR, which limits resistance due to repetition of system starting operation for a short time
COOLANT HEAT	Inverter coolant forecast temperature rose above 65℃ (149°F)	Limited power from vehicle	
CONVERTER HEAT	Boost converter temperature rose above 111℃ (232°F)	Limited power from vehicle	
SHIFT P IN RUN	Shifted to Park while driving	Vehicle went into Neutral	Vehicle will automatically shift into Neutral when the Park button is pressed while driving over 3mph
BKWRD DIR SHIFT	Shifted to R while moving forward or to D or B while moving in reverse	Vehicle went into Neutral	Vehicle will automatically shift into Neutral when another shift position is selected while moving over 3mph
PREVENT STAYING	Engine speed stays in resonance frequency band		

A.3 丰田普锐斯混合动力控制系统数据流 (Table A.3)

Table A.3 Toyota Prius Hybrid Control System Data List

Hand-held Tester Display	Measurement item/Range (Display)	Reference Range	Diagnostic Note
COOLANT TEMP	Engine coolant temperature/ Min.: −40℃, Max.: 140℃	After warming up: 80 to 100℃ (176 to 6 212°F)	• If the value is −40℃ (−40°F): Open in sensor circuit • If the value is 140 ℃ (284℃): Short in sensor circuit
VEHICLE SPD	Vehicle speed/ Min.: 0 km/h, Max.: 255 km/h	Vehicle stopped: 0 km/h (0 mph)	—
ENG RUN TIME	Elapsed time after starting engine/ Min.: 0 s, Max.: 65535 s	—	—
+B	Auxiliary battery voltage/ Min.: 0 V, Max.: 65535 V	Constant: Auxiliary battery voltage 3 V	—
ACCEL POS #1	Accelerator pedal position sensor No. 1/ Min.: 0 %, Max.: 100 %	Accelerator pedal depressed: Changes with accelerator pedal pressure	—
ACCEL POS #2	Accelerator pedal position sensor No. 2/ Min.: 0 %, Max.: 100 %	Accelerator pedal depressed: Changes with accelerator pedal pressure	—
AMBIENT TEMP	Ambient air temperature/ Min.: −40℃, Max.: 215℃	Power switch ON (IG): Same as ambient air temperature	—
INTAKE AIR TEMP	Intake air temperature/ Min.: −40 C, Max.: 140 C	Constant: Auxiliary battery voltage 3 V	—
DTC CLEAR WARM	The number of times engine is warmed up after clearing DTCs/ Min.: 0, Max.: 255	MIL OFF, engine coolant temperature increases from below 22° C (71.6° F) before starting the engine to above 70° C (158° F) after starting the engine: increases once	—

(续)

Hand-held Tester Display	Measurement item/Range (Display)	Reference Range	Diagnostic Note
DTC CLEAR RUN	Drive distance after clearing DTCs/ Min.: 0 km, Max.: 65535 km	—	—
DTC CLEAR MIN	Elapsed time after clearing DTCs/ Min.: 0 min, Max.: 65535 min	—	—
MIL ON RUN DIST	Drive distance after maifunction Occurrence/ Min.: 0 km, Max.: 65535 km	—	—
MIL ON ENG TIME	Elapsed time ater starting engine with MIL ON/ Min.: 0 min, Max.: 65535 min	—	—
MIL Status	MIL status/ ON or OFF	MIL ON: ON	Constant ON: Repair in accordance with detected DTCs
MG2 REV	MG2 revolution/ Min.: −16383 rpm, Max.: 16383 rpm	—	—
MG2 TORQ	MG2 torgue/ Min.: −500N·m, Max.: 500N·m	—	—
MG2 TRQ EXC VAL	MG2 torque execution value/ Min.: −512 N·m, Max.: 508 N·m	After full-load acceleration with READY lamp ON and engine stopped: Less than ±20 % of MG2 TORQ	—

(续)

Hand-held Tester Display	Measurement item/Range (Display)	Reference Range	Diagnostic Note
MG1 REV	MG1 revolution/ Min.: -16383 rpm, Max.: 16383 rpm	—	—
MG1 TORQ	MG1 toraue/ Min.: -500 N·m, Max.: 500 N·m	—	—
MG1 TRQ EXC VAL	MG1 torque execution value/ Min.: -512 N·m, Max.: 508 N·m	1 second has elapsed after the engine was started automatically with READY lamp ON, engine stopped, A/C fan Hi, head lamp ON and the P position: Less than ±20 % of MG1 TORQ	—
REGEN EXEC TORQ	Regenerative brake execution torque/ Min.: 0 N·m, Max.: 186 N·m	—	—
REGEN RQST TORQ	Regenerative brake request torque/ Min.: 0N·m, Max.: 186 N·m	Vehicle speed 30 km/h (19 mph) and master cylinder hydraulic pressure -200 N·m: Changes with brake pedal pressure	—
MG1 INVERT TEMP	MG1 inverter temperature/ Min.: -50℃, Max.: 205℃	• Undisturbed for 1 day at 25℃ (77°F): 25℃ (77°F) • Street driving: 25 to 80℃ (77 to 176°F)	• If the value is -50℃ (-58°F): +B short in sensor circuit • If the value is 205°C (401°F): Open or GND short in sensor circuit
MG2 INVERT TEMP	MG2 inverter temperature/ Min.: -50℃, Max.: 205℃	• Undisturbed for 1 day at 25℃ (77°F): 25℃ (77°F) • Street driving: 25 to 80℃ (77 to 176°F)	• If the value is -50℃ (-58°F): +B short in sensor circuit • If the value is 205°C (401°F): Open or GND short in sensor circuit

(续)

Hand-held Tester Display	Measurement item/Range (Display)	Reference Range	Diagnostic Note
MOTOR2 TEMP	Transaxle fuid temperature/ Min.: −50℃, Max.: 205℃	• Undisturbed for 1 day at 25℃ (77°F): 25℃ (77°F) • Street driving: 25 to 80℃ (77 to 176°F)	• If the value is −50℃ (−58°F): Open or +B short in sensor circuitt • If the value is 205°C (401°F): GND short in sensor circuit
MOTOR1 TEMP	MG2 motor temperature/ Min.: −50℃, Max.: 205℃	• Undisturbed for 1 day at 25℃ (77°F): 25℃ (77°F) • Street driving: 25 to 80℃ (77 to 176°F)	• If the value is −50℃ (−58°F): Open or +B short in sensor circuitt • If the value is 205°C (401°F): GND short in sensor circuit
CONVERTER TEMP	Boost converter temperature/ Min.: −50℃, Max.: 205℃	• Undisturbed for 1 day at 25℃ (77°F): 25℃ (77°F) • Street driving: 25 to 80℃ (77 to 140°F)	• If the value is −50℃ (−58°F): +B short in sensor circuit • If the value is 205°C (401°F): Open or GND short in sensor circuit
ACCEL DEG	Accelerator pedal depressed anglel/ Min.: 0%, Max.: 100%	Accelerator pedal depressed: Changes with accelerator pedal pressure	—
POWER RQST	Engine power output request value/ Min.: 0 W, Max.: 320000 W	—	—
TARGET ENG SPD	Target engine speed/ Min.: 0 rpm, Max.: 8000 rpm	—	—
ENGINE SPD	Engine speed/ Min.: 0 rpm, Max.: 8000 rpm	Idling *: 950 to 1050 rpm	—

(续)

Hand-held Tester Display	Measurement item/Range (Display)	Reference Range	Diagnostic Note
VEHICLE SPD	Resolver vehicle speed/ Min.: -256 km/h, Max.: 254 km/h	Driving at 40 km/h (25 mph): 40 km/h (25 mph)	—
MCYL CTRL POWER	Braking torque that is equivalent to the master cylinder hydraulic pressure/ Min.: -512N·m, Max.: 205 N·m	Brake pedal depressed: Changes with brake pedal pressure	—
SOC	Battery state of charge/ Min.: 0%, Max.: 100%	Constant: 0 to 100%	—
WOUT CTRL POWER	Discharge control power value/ Min.: 0 W, Max.: 81600 W	21000 W or less	—
WIN CTRL POWER	Charge control power value/ Min.: -40800 W, Max.: 0 W	-25000 W or more	—
DCHG RQST SOC	Discharge request to adjust SOC/ Min.: -20480 W, Max.: 20320 W	• Uniform on-board charging: -4400 W • Usually: 0 W	—
PWR RESOURCE VB	HV battery current/ Min.: 0 V, Max.: 510 V	READY lamp ON and P position: 150 to 300 V	—
PWR RESOURCE IB	HV battery current/ Min.: -256 A, Max.: 254 A	—	—
VL	High voltage before it is boosted/ Min.: 0 V, Max.: 510 V	Power switch ON (READY): Practically the same as the HV battery voltage	• If the value is 0 V: Open or GND short in sensor circuit • If the value is 510 V: +B short in sensor circuit

(续)

Hand-held Tester Display	Measurement item/Range (Display)	Reference Range	Diagnostic Note
VH	High voltage before it is boosted/ Min.: 0 V, Max.: 765 V	Engine revved up in P position; HV battery voltage to 500 V	• If the value is 0 V: Open or GND short in sensor circuit • If the value is 765 V: +B short in sensor circuit
RAIS PRES RATIO	Boost ratio/ Min.: 0%, Max.: 100%	The pre-boost voltage and the post-boost voltage are equal: 0 to 10%	—
DRIVE CONDITION	Drive condition ID/ Min: 0, Max.: 6	• Engine stopped: 0 • Engine about to be stopped: 1 • Engine about to be started: 2 • Enging operated or operating: 3 • Generating or loading movement: 4 • Revving up with P position: 6	—
M SHIFT SENSOR	Output voltage of the shift position sensor (main)/ Min.: 0 V, Max.: 5 V	• Selector lever in home position: 2.0 to 3.0 V • Shifting into R position: 4.0 to 4.8 V • Shifting into B or D position: 0.2 to 1.0 V	—
S SHIFT SENSOR	Output voltage of the shift position sensor (sub)/ Min.: 0 V, Max.: 5 V	• Selector lever in home position: 2.0 to 3.0 V • Shifting into R position: 4.0 to 4.8 V • Shifting into B or D position: 0.2 to 1.0 V	—
SM SHIFT SENSOR	Output voltage of the select position sensor (main)/ Min.: 0 V, Max.: 5 V	• Selector lever in home position: 0.5 to 2.0 V • Shifting into R, N or D position: 3.0 to 4.85 V	—

(续)

Hand-held Tester Display	Measurement item/Range (Display)	Reference Range	Diagnostic Note
SS SHIFT SENSOR	Output voltage of the select position sensor (sub) / Min.: 0 V, Max.: 5 V	• Selector lever in home position: 0.5 to 2.0 V • Shifting into R, N or D position: 3.0 to 4.85 V	—
SHIFT POSITION	Shift position	P, R, N, D or B	—
CRANK POS	Crankshaft position/ Min.: −90 deg, Max.: 90 deg	—	—
A/C CONSMPT PWR	A/C consumption power/ Min.: 0 kW, Max.: −5 kW	—	—
DRIVE CONDITION	Driving condition	• MG1 load: MG1 • MG2 load: MG2	—
SHORT WAVE HIGH	Waveform voltage in leak detection circuit in battery ECU/ Min.: 0 V, Max.: 5 V	READY lamp is left ON for 2 minutes, and the pre-boost voltage and the post-boost voltage are equal: 4 V or more	—
MG1 CTRL MODE	MG1 control mode/ ON or OFF	—	—
MG1 CARRIR FREQ	MG1 carrier frequency/5 kHz or 10 kHz	—	—
MG2 CTRL MODE	MG2 control mode/ ON or OFF	—	—
MG2 CARRIR FREQ	MG2 carrier frequency/1.25 kHz or 5 kHz	—	—
ECU TYPE	Type of ECU	HV ECU	—

(续)

Hand-held Tester Display	Measurement item/Range (Display)	Reference Range	Diagnostic Note
CURRENT DTC	The number of current DTCs/ Min.: 0, Max.: 255	—	—
HISTORY DTC	The number of history DTCs/ Min.: 0, Max.: 255	—	—
CHECK MODE	Check mode/ON or OFF	—	—
ENG STOP RQST	Engine stop request/NO or RQST	Requesting engine stop: RQST	—
IDLING REQUEST	Engine idling request/NO or RQST	Requesting idle: RQST	—
HV BATT CH RQST	HV battery charging request/NO or RQST	Requesting HV battery charging: RQST	—
ENG STP INHIBIT	Engine stop inhibit request/NO or RQST	Requesting engine intermittent prohibition: RQST	—
AIR CON REQUEST	Engine starting request from A/C amplifier/NO or RQST	Requesting engine start from A/C amplifier: RQST	—
ENG WARM UP RQST	Engine warm-up request/NO or RQST	Requesting engine warm-up: RQST	—
SMR CONT1	Operating condition of system main relay No.1/ON or OFF	Power switch ON (READY): OFF	—
SMR CONT2	Operating condition of system main relay No.2/ ON or OFF	Power switch ON (READY): ON	—

(续)

Hand-held Tester Display	Measurement item/Range (Display)	Reference Range	Diagnostic Note
SMR CONT3	Operating condition of system main relay No. 3 ON or OFF	Power switch ON (READY): ON	—
MG1 GATE	MG1 gate status/ON or OFF	ON	—
MG2 GATE	MG2 gate status/ON or OFF	Shutting down motor inverter: ON	—
CNV GATE	Boost converter gate status/ON or OFF	Shutting down boost converter: ON	—
A/C GATE	A/C gate status/ON or OFF	Shutting down A/C inverter: ON	—
SMARTKEY	Electronic key ID code check status/ON or OFF	When electronic key ID code corresponds to ID code registered in ECU: ON	—
CNV CARRIER FREQ	Boost converter carrier frequency/ 5 kHz or 10 kHz	—	—

附录 B 常用汽车英语缩写与含义

缩写	英文含义	中文含义
2WD	two wheel drive	两轮驱动
4WD	four wheel drive	四轮驱动
4WS	four wheel steering	四轮转向
A/C	air conditioning	空调
A/C	air cleaner	空气滤清器
A/F	air/fuel ratio	空燃比
ABC	active body control	车身主动控制
ABD	automatic braking-force distribution	制动力自动分配
ABDC	after bottom dead center	下止点后
ABS	antilock braking system	防抱死制动系统
AC	alternating current	交流电
AC	air conditioning, air cleaner	空调, 空气滤清器
ACC	accessory	附件
ACC	adaptive cruise control	自适应巡航控制
ACIM	AC induction motor	交流感应式电机
ACS	automatic clutch system	离合器自动操纵系统
AD	analogue-digital (converter)	模-数（转换器）
AER	all-electric-range	全电行驶续驶里程
ALSD	automatic limited-slip differential	自动防滑差速器
ALT	alternator	发电机
AMT	automated manual transmission	机械式自动变速器
API	American petroleum institute	美国石油学会
ASC	anti-stability control	稳定性自动控制
ASCD	automatic speed control system	自动车速控制系统
ASR	anti-slip regulation	加速防滑调节（系统）
AT	automatic transmission	自动变速器
AT	automatic transaxle	自动变速驱动桥
ATF	automatic transmission fluid	自动变速器油
ATS	adaptive transmission control	自适应变速器控制
AUX	auxiliary	辅助

（续）

缩写	英文含义	中文含义
AVG	average	平均
AWD	all-wheel drive	全轮驱动
BA	brake assist	制动辅助
BAS	brake assistant system	制动辅助系统
BAT	battery	蓄电池
BATT	battery	蓄电池
BBDC	before bottom dead center	下止点前
BDC	bottom dead centre	下止点
BEAN	body electronic area network	车身电控局域网
BEV	battery electric vehicle	纯电动汽车
BMS	battery management system	电池管理系统
CA	crankshaft angle	曲轴转角
CAN	controller area network	控制器局域网
CB	circuit breaker	电路断电器
CBS	combined brake system	组合制动系统
CC	cruise control	巡航控制
CCS	cruise control system	巡航控制系统
CDI	capacitive discharge ignition	电容放电点火
CE	combustion engine	内燃机
CFRP	carbon-fiber-reinforced plastic	碳纤维增强塑料
CI	compression ignition	压燃式
CKP	crankshaft position	曲轴位置
CMP	camshaft position	凸轮轴位置
CN	cetane number	十六烷值
CNG	compressed natural gas	压缩天然气
CPS	crankshaft position sensor	曲轴位置传感器
CPU	central processing unit	中央处理单元
CR	common rail	共轨（油管）
CR	compression ratio	压缩比
CARB	California Air Resources Board	加利福尼亚大气资源局
CS	camshaft	凸轮轴
CV	control valve	控制阀
CV	commercial vehicle	商用车

（续）

缩写	英文含义	中文含义
CV	check valve	单向阀
CVT	continuous variable transmission	机械式无级变速器
D	drive	驱动
DA	drive axle	驱动桥
DC	direct current	直流（电）
DC-DC		直流－直流
DCT	dual clutch transmission	双离合变速器
DEF	defogger	除雾器
DI	direct injection	直喷
DLC3	data link connector 3	3号诊断插座
DME	digital motor electronics	数字式发动机电控装置
DMM	digital multimeter	数字式万用表
DOD	depth of discharge	放电深度
DOHC	double overhead camshaft	双顶置凸轮轴
DOT	Department of Transport	运输部
DRL	day running light	日间行车灯
DSC	dynamic stability control	动态稳定性控制
DSG	direct shift gearbox	直接换档变速器
DSP	dynamic shift-program	动态换档程序
DTC	diagnostic tester code	故障码
DVOM	digital volt/ohm meter	数字式万用表
EBD	electronic brake distribution	电子控制制动力分配
EBS	electronic braking system	电子控制制动系统
ECC	electronic climate control	电子控制气候控制
ECE	Economic Commission for Europe	欧洲经济委员会
ECM	engine control module	发动机控制模块
ECM	electronic control module	电子控制模块
ECM	electronic clutch management	离合器电子管理
ECS	electronic clutch system	离合器电子控制系统
ECT	electronic control transmission	电子控制变速器
ECU	electronic control unit	电子控制单元
EDC	electronic diesel control	柴油机电子控制
EEPROM	electrically erasable programmable read-only memory	电可擦可编程只读存储器

（续）

缩写	英文含义	中文含义
E-gas	electronic throttle control	电子节气门
EGR	exhaust gas recirculation	废气再循环
EGS	electronic gearbox control	变速器电子控制
EHB	electro-hydraulic braking system	电-液自动系统
EI	emissions inspection	排放检测
ELSD	electronic limited-slip differential	电子控制限滑差速器
EM	electric motor	电动机
EMC	electro-magnetic compatibility	电磁兼容性
EMS	electronic engine management system	发动机电子管理系统
ENG	engine	发动机
EOBD	European on-board diagnosis	欧洲车载诊断
EPA	the United States Environmental Protection Agency	美国环保署
EPA	Environmental Protection Agency	美国环保署
EPHS	electrically powered hydraulic steering	电动液压转向
EPS	electro-pneumatic control system	电-气动控制系统
EPS	electric power steering	电动转向
ESP	electronic stability program	电子稳定性程序
ESS	energy storage system	储能系统
ETC	electronic throttle control	电子节气门控制
ETC	electronic temperature control	电子温度控制
ETCS-i	electronic throttle control system with intelligence	智能型节气门电子控制
EV	electric vehicle	电动汽车
EV	exhaust valve	排气门
EVAP	evaporative emission	蒸发排放
FA	front axle	前桥
FC	fuel cell	燃料电池
FCEV	fuel cell electric vehicle	燃料电池电动汽车
FCHEV	fuel cell hybrid electric vehicle	燃料电池混合动力汽车
FDI	fuel direct injection	燃料直接喷射
FE	fuel economy	燃料经济性
FFV	flexible fuel vehicles	灵活燃料汽车
FL	front left	左前
FL	fusible link	易熔线

（续）

缩写	英文含义	中文含义
FR	front right	右前
FSI	fuel stratified injection	燃料分层喷射
FWD	four wheel drive	前轮驱动
GDI	gasoline direct injection	汽油直喷
GFRP	glass-fibre-reinforced plastic	玻璃纤维增强塑料
GND	ground	搭铁，接地
GPS	global positioning sensor	全球定位传感器
GVWR	gross vehicle weight rating	汽车总重量
HCAC	hydrocarbon absorption catalyst	碳氢化合物吸收催化剂
HEV	hybrid electric vehicle	混合动力汽车
HF	high frequency	高频
HF	hybridization factor	混合度
H-Fuse	high current fuse	大电流熔断器
HGV	heavy goods vehicle	重型货车
HV	hybrid vehicle	混合动力汽车
HV	high voltage	高压
IAC	idle air control	怠速控制
IAT	intake air temperature	进气温度
IC	internal combustion	内燃
IC	integrated circuit	集成电路
ICE	internal combustion engine	内燃机
ICEV	internal combustion engine vehicle	内燃机汽车
IDI	indirect injection	间接喷射
IG	ignition	点火，点火开关
IGBT	insulated gate bipolar transistor	绝缘栅双极晶体管
IMA	integrated motor assist	集成化电机辅助
INT	instrument panel	仪表板
IPM	interior permanent magnet	内置永磁
IPU	intelligent power unit	智能动力单元
IS	input shaft	输入轴
IV	inlet valve	进气门
LED	light emitting diode	发光二极管
LEV	low-emission vehicle	低排放汽车

（续）

缩写	英文含义	中文含义
LF	low frequency	低频
Li-ion	lithium-ion（battery）	锂离子（电池）
LIN	local interconnect network	局域互联网
Li-poly	lithium-polymer（battery）	锂-聚合物（电池）
LLC	long life coolant	长寿命冷却液
LNG	liquefied natural gas	液化天然气
LOI	loss of insulation	绝缘损耗，绝缘破坏
LPG	liquid petroleum gas	液化石油气
LSG	laminated safety glass	层压安全玻璃
M/T	manual transmission	手动变速器
MAF	mass air flow	质量空气流量
MAX	maximum	最大
MCM	motor control module	电机控制模块
MDM	motor drive module	电机驱动模块
ME	motor electronics	发电机控制电子装置
MEA	membrane electrode assembly	膜电极
MED	motor electronics direct injection	汽油直喷发动机电子控制
MG	motor generator	电动机/发电机
MGR	motor/generator rear	电动机/发电机（后）
mi	mile	英里
MIL	malfunction indicator lamp	故障指示灯
MIN	minimum	最小
MON	motor-octane number	马达法辛烷值
MPG/mpg	miles per gallon	英里/加仑
MPGe	miles per gallon equivalent	当量英里/加仑
MPI	multi-point injection	多点喷射
MT	manual transmission	手动变速器
N	neutral	空档
Ni-Cd	nickel-cadmium（battery）	镍-镉（电池）
NiMH	nickel-metal hydride（battery）	镍-氢（电池）
NTC	negative temperature coefficient	负温度系数
O/D	overdrive	超速档，超速传动

(续)

缩写	英文含义	中文含义
OBD	on-board diagnosis	车载诊断
OD	overdrive	超速档，超速传动
OHC	over-head camshaft	顶置凸轮轴
OHV	over-head valves	顶置气门
ON	octane number	辛烷值
OS	output shaft	输出轴
OSHA	the Occupational Safety and Health Administration	美国职业安全与健康管理局
P	park	驻车档
PCM	powertrain control module	动力控制模块
PCS	power control system	动力控制系统
PCU	power control unit	动力控制单元
PCV	positive crankshaft ventilation	曲轴箱强制通风
PDU	power drive unit	动力驱动单元
PEM	proton exchange membrane	质子交换膜
PEMFC	proton exchange membrane fuel cell	质子交换膜燃料电池
PEV	plug-in electric vehicle	插电式电动汽车
PHEV	plug-in hybrid electric vehicle	插电式混合动力汽车
PID	parameter identification	参数识别
PM	permanent magnet	永磁
PM	particulate matter	颗粒物
PNGV	the Partnership for a New Generation of Vehicles	新一代汽车合作开发计划
PR	ply rating	层级
PS	power steering	动力转向
PSM	permanent magnet three-phase synchronous motor	永磁三相交流同步电机
PTC	positive temperature coefficient	正温度系数
PTO	power take-off	取力器，动力输出装置
PWM	pulse width modulation	脉宽调制
QA	quality assurance	质量保证
QM	quality management	质量管理
R	reverse	倒档，倒车
RA	rear axle	后桥
RAM	random access memory	随机存取存储器
RBS	regenerative brake system	再生制动系统

(续)

缩写	英文含义	中文含义
RHD	right-hand drive	右侧驾驶
RL	rear left	左后
RLFS	return-less-fuel system	无回油燃油供给系统
RLY	relay	继电器
RON	research-octane number	研究法辛烷值
ROP	roll-over protection	侧翻保护
RR	rear right	右后
RWD	rear wheel drive	后轮驱动
SAC	self-adjusting clutch	自行调节离合器
SAE	Society of Automotive Engineers	美国汽车工程师学会
SCR	selective catalytic reduction	选择催化还原
SCV	solenoid control valve	控制电磁阀
SEFI	sequential electronic fuel injection	电控顺序燃油喷射
SEN	sensor	传感器
SFI	sequential multiport fuel injection	顺序多点燃油喷射
SI	spark ignition	点燃式
SLLC	super long life coolant	超长寿命冷却液
SMR	system main relay	系统主继电器
SOC	state of charge	荷电状态
SOH	state of health	健康状态
SOHC	single overhead camshaft	单顶置凸轮轴
SPI	single-point injection	单点喷射
SPM	surface permanent magnet	表面永磁
SRS	safety restraint systems	约束保护安全系统
SRS	supplemental restraint system	补充乘员约束保护系统
SSR	self-supporting run-flat tyre	自行支撑式泄气保用胎（防爆胎）
SST	special service tool	专用维修工具
ST	scan tool	扫描工具
SUV	sport utility vehicle	运动型多用途车
SV	solenoid valve	电磁阀
SW	switch	开关
TACH	tachometer	转速表
TB	throttle body	节气门

(续)

缩写	英文含义	中文含义
TCM	transmission control module	变速器控制模块
TCS	traction control system	牵引力控制系统
TDC	top dead centre	上止点
THS	Toyota hybrid system	丰田混合动力系统
TIS	Toyota information system	丰田信息系统
TL	tubeless	无内胎
TP	throttle position	节气门位置
TPC	tire-pressure check	轮胎压力检查
TPS	throttle position sensor	节气门位置传感器
TRAC	traction control system	牵引力控制系统
TSB	technical service bulletin	技术服务公报
TWC	three way catalytic converter	三元催化转化器
TWI	tread wear indicator	轮胎花纹磨损指示器
UIS	unit injector system	泵喷嘴系统
ULEV	ultra low emissions-vehicle	超低排放车辆
UPS	unit pump system	单体泵系统
VDC	vehicle dynamics controller	车辆动态控制器
VF	variable focus (reflector)	可变焦点（反射镜）
VHF	very high frequency	甚高频
VIN	vehicle identification number	车辆识别号
VPS	vapor pressure sensor	蒸汽压力传感器
VSC	vehicle stability control	车辆稳定性控制
VSS	vehicle speed sensor	车速传感器
VSV	vacuum switching valve	真空开关阀
VTEC	variable valve timing and lift electronic control	可变气门定时与升程电子控制
VTG	variable turbine geometry	可调涡轮几何
VVT-i	variable valve timing with intelligence	智能型可变气门定时
w	with	带有
w/o	without	没有
WOT	wide open throttle	节气门全开
ZEV	zero emissions vehicle	零排放车辆

附录 C 常用汽车专业术语

英文含义	中文含义	出现章节
AC induction motor（ACIM）	交流感应电机	3.2
acceleration time	加速时间	7.3
active test	主动测试	6.2
aerodynamic drag force	空气阻力	7.3
air line	空气管路	8.1
alkaline battery	碱性电池	2.2
alkaline fuel cell	碱性燃料电池	8.1
all-electric-range（AER）	全电续驶里程	1.3
all-wheel drive	全轮驱动	4.2
alternative fuel	替代燃料	1.1
alternative fueled vehicle	替代燃料汽车	1.1
ampere-hour（A·h）capacity	安·时容量	2.1
armature winding	电枢绕组	3.1
asynchronous AC motor	交流异步电机	3.1
automatic transmission	自动变速器	4.2
auxiliary battery	辅助蓄电池	2.2
balancing unit	平衡装置	2.3
battery block	电池块，电池子模块	2.5
battery controller	蓄电池控制器	2.3
battery electric vehicle（BEV）	纯电动汽车	1.3
battery management system（BMS）	电池管理系统（BMS）	2.3
battery pack	电池组	1.3
bell-shaped housing	钟形壳	4.2
bench seat	长条座椅	5.3
bipolar plate	双极板	8.1
bivalent drive	双元驱动	9.1
block diagram	框图	2.3
boost converter	升压变换器	3.3
braking effort	制动力	5.3
BTU	英国热量单位（=252cal）	5.1

(续)

英文含义	中文含义	出现章节
burst pressure	爆裂压力	9.2
cabin air	车内空气	2.3
calendar life	历年寿命	2.1
calorific value	热值	9.1
Car of the Year	年度最佳汽车	5.2
carbon dioxide	二氧化碳	9.1
carbon paper	碳纸，复写纸	8.1
CE	内燃机	4.2
cell controller	单体电池控制器	2.3
CFRP	碳纤维增强塑料	9.2
charge state	荷电状态	4.2
charging rate	充电率，充电速度	2.4
chemical reaction equation	化学反应方程	2.2
chemical reforming	化学重整	8.2
city bus	城市公共汽车	2.1
clamping-ring	夹紧环	9.2
climbing resistive force	爬坡阻力	7.3
CNG	压缩天然气	1.1
combustion chamber	燃烧室	9.2
combustion property	燃烧特性	9.1
come in [into] to contact with	接触到	2.5
commutator segment	换向器片	3.2
compressed natural gas	压缩天然气	1.2
compression ignition engine	压燃式发动机	1.2
compression ratio	压缩比	5.3
continuously variable transmission	机械式无级变速器	4.2
curb weight	整备质量	5.3
current driver	电流驱动器	3.3
current-carrying conductor	载流导体	3.2
cycle life	循环寿命	2.1
DC-DC converter	直流-直流变换器	1.3
deep-cycle battery	深度循环蓄电池	2.1
depth of discharge (DOD)	放电深度	2.1

（续）

英文含义	中文含义	出现章节
design parameter	设计参数	7.3
diagnostic trouble code	故障码	3.4
diesel fuel	柴油燃料	1.2
digital multimeter (DMM)	数字式万用表	3.4
diode bridge	二极管电桥	2.4
discharge rate	放电率	7.2
double-layer capacitor	双层电容器	2.1
drag torque	反拖力矩	4.2
drive force	驱动力	5.3
drive train	传动系统	1.3
drive wheel	驱动车轮，驱动轮	7.1
driver circuit	驱动电路	3.3
driving range	续驶里程	1.3
DSG gearbox	双离合变速器	5.3
dual fuel	双燃料（汽车）	1.2
dual mass flywheel	双质量飞轮	4.2
electric drive motor	驱动电机	3.3
electric motor	电机	1.1
electric starter	起动机	1.1
electric vehicle	电动汽车	1.1
electrical machine	电机	2.1
electrical schematic	电气原理图，电气简图	6.1
electric-powered vehicle	电动汽车	1.1
electromagnetic induction	电磁感应	3.2
electronic fuel injection	电子控制燃料喷射	5.3
electronic switch	电子开关	3.2
electronic throttle	电子节气门	5.3
enable circuit	使能电路	3.4
energy accumulator	蓄能器，储能系统	2.1
energy density	能量密度	1.2
energy storage	储能（装置）	4.2
energy storage system (ESS)	储能系统	8.2
energy storage unit	储能装置	1.3

(续)

英文含义	中文含义	出现章节
E-REV	增程式电动汽车	1.1
excitation current	励磁电流	3.1
fatigue failure	疲劳失效	9.2
fiberglass pole	玻璃纤维杆	6.1
field coil	励磁绕组，磁场绕组	3.2
field winding	磁场绕组	3.1
fire extinguisher	灭火器	2.5
fire fighter	消防员	2.5
fixed-ratio reduction gear	固定速比减速机构	7.1
flexible fuel vehicles（FFV）	灵活燃料汽车	1.2
flux leakage	漏磁	2.4
fossil fuel	化石燃料，矿物燃料	9.1
freeze frame	冻结数据帧	6.2
front-wheel drive	前轮驱动	4.2
fuel consumption	耗油率，燃料消耗	5.3
fuel economy	燃料经济性	4.1
fuel efficiency	燃料经济性，燃料效率	1.3
fuel tank	燃料箱	2.1
fuel-cell car	燃料电池汽车	1.2
fuel-cell electric vehicles（FCEV）	燃料电池电动汽车	1.3
fuel-cell stack	燃料电池堆	8.1
full electric vehicle	纯电动汽车	1.3
full face shield	全面罩	6.1
full hybrid	重度混合动力	4.1
gas injector	气体喷射器	9.2
gas-leak detector	气体泄漏检测器，检漏仪	9.3
gasoline engine	汽油机	1.1
gasoline-electric hybrid automobile	油电混合动力汽车	1.1
gas-pressure regulator	气压调节器	9.2
gear box	齿轮箱	7.1
gear unit	齿轮机构	4.2
greenhouse gas	温室气体	1.2
Hall-effect sensor	霍尔效应传感器	3.2

（续）

英文含义	中文含义	出现章节
hand crank	起动摇把	1.1
hand-held tester	手持式检测仪	6.2
heat sink	散热片	3.4
hill-climbing capability	爬坡能力	7.1
horseless carriage	无马的马车，老式汽车	1.1
hub-reduction gear set	轮毂减速机构	5.3
HV battery pack	高压电池组	2.3
hybrid car	混合动力汽车	1.1
hybrid drive	混合动力，混合驱动装置	4.1
hybrid electric vehicles（HEV）	混合动力电动汽车	1.3
hybrid module	混合动力模块	4.2
hybridization factor	混合度	4.1
hydraulic accumulator	液压蓄能器	2.1
hydrogen fuel cell	氢燃料电池	1.1
hydrogen fueling station	加氢站	1.3
IC engine	内燃机	2.2
individual cell	单体电池	8.1
industrial truck	工业车辆	2.2
in-hull drive	船体内驱动	7.1
input shaft	输入轴	4.2
instrument cluster	组合仪表	5.3
insulated gate bipolar transistor（IGBT）	绝缘栅双极晶体管	3.3
insulation resistance	绝缘电阻	6.1
integrated motor assist（IMA）	集成化电机辅助	4.2
intelligent power unit（IPU）	智能动力单元	4.2
interior permanent magnet（IPM）	内部永磁	3.2
inverter combustion engine	发动机	3.1
inverter assembly	逆变器总成	3.3
kinetic energy	动能	4.2
knock resistance	抗爆性	9.1
lead-acid battery	铅酸蓄电池	2.1
life cycle	生命周期	5.1
liquefied natural gas	液化天然气	9.1

(续)

英文含义	中文含义	出现章节
liquefied petroleum gas	液化石油气	1.2
lithium battery	锂电池	2.1
lithium cobalt oxide	钴酸锂（$LiCoO_2$）	2.2
lithium iron phosphate	磷酸铁锂（$LiFePO_4$）	2.2
lithium nickel cobalt manganate	三元锂（镍钴锰酸锂）（$LiNiCoMnO_2$）	2.2
lithium-ion battery	锂离子电池	1.1
lithium-polymer battery	锂聚合物电池	2.1
litmus paper	石蕊试纸	2.5
lockup clutch	锁止离合器	5.3
loss of insulation	绝缘损耗	6.1
low-rate limiter	流量限制器	9.2
luxury car	豪华汽车	5.2
magnetic field	磁场	3.2
make electrical contact with	与……电接触	3.2
market niche	市场定位，商机	4.1
medium hybrid	中度混合动力	4.1
megger tester	绝缘测试仪	6.2
membrane electrode assembly（MEA）	膜电极	8.1
metal hydride	金属氢化物	2.2
micro hybrid	微混合动力	4.1
mild hybrid	轻度混合动力	4.1
miles per gallon（MPG）	英里/加仑	5.1
miles per gallon equivalent（MPGe）	当量英里/加仑	5.1
Miller cycle	米勒循环	5.3
molten carbonate fuel cell	熔融碳酸盐燃料电池	8.1
motor control module（MCM）	电机控制模块	3.3
motor controller	电机控制器	3.3
motor drive module（MDM）	电机驱动模块	4.2
motor generator（MG）	电动机/发电机总成	6.2
motor inverter	电机逆变器	1.3
motor vehicle	汽车，机动车	3.1
moving-off element	移离元件，起步元件	4.2
multimedia infotainment display	多媒体信息娱乐显示器	5.3

(续)

英文含义	中文含义	出现章节
multi-plate clutch	多片离合器	4.2
negative electrode	负极	2.2
nickel-metal hydride battery pack	镍氢电池组	1.1
nickel-based battery	镍电池	2.1
nickel-cadmium (Ni-Cd) battery	镍镉(Ni-Cd)电池	2.2
nickel-metal hydride (NiMH) battery	镍氢(NiMH)电池	2.2
off-board charging	离车充电	2.4
ohmic loss	电阻损耗	3.1
oil crisis	石油危机	1.1
onboard charging	车载充电,随车充电	2.4
open circuit	断路	6.2
operating condition	工作条件,工作状况	2.1
overpressure regulator	过压调节器	9.2
oxidation-reduction reaction	氧化还原反应	2.2
parallel hybrid	并联式混合动力	4.1
parking space	停车位	2.4
passenger vehicle	乘用车,载客车辆	3.1
performance objective	性能目标	7.2
performance parameter	性能参数	7.2
permanent magnet	永久磁铁	3.1
permanent magnet brushless DC motor	永磁无刷直流电机	3.2
personal protective equipment (PPE)	人身保护设备	2.5
petrol engine	汽油机	5.3
phosphoric acid fuel cell	磷酸燃料电池	8.1
pinpoint test	详细测试	3.4
planet carrier	行星架	4.2
planetary gear set	行星齿轮机构	4.2
planetary gearbox	行星齿轮减速器	7.1
plug-in electric vehicles (PEV)	插电式电动汽车	1.3
plug-in HEV	插电式混合动力电动汽车	1.1
plug-in hybrid electric vehicle (PHEV)	插电式混合动力电动汽车	1.3
pole shoes	极靴	3.2
positive electrode	正极	2.2

（续）

英文含义	中文含义	出现章节
potassium hydroxide	氢氧化钾	2.5
power battery	动力电池	1.2
power density	功率密度	2.1
power down	断电，掉电	6.1
power drive unit（PDU）	动力驱动单元	3.3
power electronics	功率电子器件，控制器	2.4
power flow	能流	2.4
power grid	电网，电力网	1.3
power plant	发电厂，动力装置	3.1
power shifting	动力换档	7.1
power supply	供电，电源	4.2
power transistor	功率晶体管	3.3
power-split hybrid	功率分流式混合动力，混联式混合动力	4.1
prime mover	原动机，原动力，发动机	4.1
propeller shaft	传动轴	7.1
proton exchange membrane	质子交换膜	8.1
proton exchange membrane fuel cell（PEMFC）	质子交换膜燃料电池	8.1
pulse width	脉冲宽度，脉宽	3.3
pure electric vehicle	纯电动汽车	1.3
racing car	赛车	1.1
receiving coil	接收线圈	2.4
recurring check	反复检查	9.3
refuelling valve	充气阀	9.2
regenerative braking	再生制动	1.3
remaining capacity	剩余容量	2.3
rolling resistive force	滚动阻力	7.3
root cause	根本原因	3.4
safety glasses	安全眼镜	6.1
safety plug	安全插头	2.5
schematic diagram	原理图，示意图	1.3
selector transmission	选档式变速器	7.1
sensing unit	传感装置	2.3
serial hybrid	串联式混合动力	4.1

(续)

英文含义	中文含义	出现章节
series-parallel hybrid	混联式混合动力，功率分流式混合动力	4.1
series-wound DC motor	串励直流电机	3.1
service manual	维修手册	2.5
service plug	维修插头	2.5
shock hazard	电击危险	6.1
short circuit	短路，短接	6.2
shut off valve	截止阀	9.2
smart key	智能钥匙	6.2
solar energy	太阳能	1.2
solder fuse	焊料熔断器	9.2
solid oxide fuel cell	固体氧化物燃料电池	8.1
spark ignition engine	点燃式发动机	1.2
special wheeled and tracked vehicle	轮式和履带式专用车辆	7.1
special-purpose vehicle	专用车辆	7.1
specific energy	比能量	2.1
specific power	比功率	2.1
spider shaft	行星齿轮轴	4.2
squirrel-cage rotor	鼠笼式转子	3.2
stall test	失速试验	6.2
starting device	起步装置	5.3
starting torque	起动转矩	3.2
state of charge（SOC）	荷电状态	2.1
state of health（SOH）	健康状态	2.1
status circuit	状态电路	3.4
steel cylinder	钢筒，钢瓶	2.2
steering wheel	转向盘	5.3
strong hybrid	重度混合动力，强混合动力	4.1
summarising gear	合成机构	4.2
summarising gearbox	功率合成齿轮箱	7.1
surface permanent magnet（SPM）	表面永磁	3.2
synchronous AC motor	交流同步电机	3.1
take part in	参加，参与	2.2
tandem motor	级联电机，双电机	7.1

(续)

英文含义	中文含义	出现章节
technical service bulletin（TSB）	技术服务公报	6.1
temperature sensor	温度传感器	2.3
thermal cut-out	热熔熔断器	9.2
thermal energy	热能	5.3
torque converter	液力变矩器	4.2
total resistive force	总阻力	7.3
touch screen	触摸屏	5.3
traction motor	推进电机	1.3
tractive effort	驱动力	7.3
transmission system	传动系统	4.2
transmitting coil	发射线圈	2.4
transportation means	运输工具	1.2
variable valve timing intelligent	智能型可变气门定时	5.3
warning label	警告标贴	2.5
wheel hub drive	轮毂驱动	7.1
wheel motor	车轮电机	5.3
wireless charging	无线充电	2.4
wiring harness	线束	6.2
work order	工作单，工作通知单，工作订单	6.1
World Green Car of the Year	世界年度绿色汽车	5.2
wound rotor	绕线式转子	3.2
zero-emission vehicle	零排放汽车	1.3

附录 D 词汇总表（英中对照）

英文含义	音标	中文含义	出现章节
abnormality	[ˌæbnɔːˈmæləti]	n. 反常，变态	6.2
abuse	[əˈbjuːs]	n. 滥用	2.2
acceleration	[əkˌseləˈreɪʃn]	n. 加速，加速度	1.3
accelerator	[əkˈseləreɪtə(r)]	n. 加速器，节气门	5.3
acceptance	[əkˈseptəns]	n. 接受，接纳	7.2
accessory	[əkˈsesəri]	n. 附件	2.2
accommodate	[əˈkɒmədeɪt]	v. 容纳	2.1
accumulate	[əˈkjuːmjəleɪt]	vt. & vi. 堆积，积累	2.1
activation	[ˌæktɪˈveɪʃn]	n. 活化，激活	3.2
add-on	[ˈædɒn]	n. 附加物；adj. 附加的	4.2
address	[əˈdres]	n. 地址；v. 处理	1.2
adhere	[ədˈhɪə(r)]	vt. 遵循，坚持	2.5
aerodynamic	[ˌeərəʊdaɪˈnæmɪk]	adj. 空气动力（学）的	7.3
aesthetics	[iːsˈθetɪks]	n. 美学	5.3
agility	[əˈdʒɪləti]	n. 敏捷，活泼，灵活	8.2
alcohol	[ˈælkəhɒl]	n. 乙醇，酒精	1.2
alkali	[ˈælkəlaɪ]	n. 碱	2.5
alloy	[ˈælɔɪ]	n. 合金	8.1
alongside	[əˌlɒŋˈsaɪd]	adv. 与……并排；prep. 在……旁边	2.2
amplitude	[ˈæmplɪtjuːd]	n. 振幅	3.3
anode	[ˈænəʊd]	n. 阳极	2.2
anxiety	[æŋˈzaɪəti]	n. 焦虑，忧虑	1.3
approach	[əˈprəʊtʃ]	vt. & vi. 接近	3.1
appropriate	[əˈprəʊpriət]	adj. 适当的，合适的	2.5
approx.	[əˈprɒks]	adv. 大约（=approximately）	9.1
aqueous	[ˈeɪkwiəs]	adj. 水的，水成的	2.2
architecture	[ˈɑːkɪtektʃə(r)]	n. 结构	2.4
arguably	[ˈɑːgjuəbli]	adv. 可以说	5.3
armature	[ˈɑːmətʃə(r)]	n. 电枢；转子	3.1
asynchronous	[eɪˈsɪŋkrənəs]	adj. 异步的	3.1

(续)

英文含义	音标	中文含义	出现章节
atmospheric	[ˌætməsˈferɪk]	adj. 大气的	8.1
auxiliary	[ɔːgˈzɪliəri]	adj. 辅助的	2.2
badge	[bædʒ]	n. 徽章，标记	5.3
bidirectional	[ˌbaɪdəˈrekʃənl]	adj. 双向的	2.4
bivalent	[baɪˈveɪlənt]	adj. 二价的；n. 二价体	9.1
block	[blɒk]	vt. 阻止	3.4
bottleneck	[ˈbɒtlnek]	n. 瓶颈	7.2
brisk	[brɪsk]	adj. 快的，轻快的	5.3
brush	[brʌʃ]	n. 刷子，电刷	3.2
brushless	[bˈrʌʃlɪs]	adj. 无刷的	3.2
bulletin	[ˈbʊlətɪn]	n. 公告，公报	6.1
by-product	[ˈbaɪprɒdʌkt]	n. 副产品，意外结果	1.2
calculate	[ˈkælkjuleɪt]	vt. & vi. 计算，估计	2.1
calculation	[ˌkælkjuˈleɪʃn]	n. 计算	5.1
candidate	[ˈkændɪdət]	n. 候选人	1.2
carbonate	[ˈkɑːbəneɪt]	n. 碳酸盐	8.1
categorize	[ˈkætəgəraɪz]	vt. 分类	1.3
cathode	[ˈkæθəʊd]	n. 阴极	2.2
cell	[sel]	n. 电池，单体电池	2.1
characterize	[ˈkærəktəraɪz]	vt. 描述……的特性	2.1
charge	[tʃɑːdʒ]	vt. 充电；n. 电荷	1.3
charger	[ˈtʃɑːdʒə(r)]	n. 充电器，增压器	1.3
chase	[tʃeɪs]	vi. 追逐，追赶	3.2
coasting	[ˈkəʊstɪŋ]	n. 滑行	4.2
collector	[kəˈlektə(r)]	n. 集电极	3.3
communicate	[kəˈmjuːnɪkeɪt]	vi. 通信，相连，互通	2.3
commutation	[ˌkɒmjuˈteɪʃn]	n. 换向	3.1
commutator	[ˈkɒmjuteɪtə(r)]	n. 换向器	3.2
comparable	[ˈkɒmpərəbl]	adj. 可比较的，比得上的	7.2
comparison	[kəmˈpærɪsn]	n. 比较，对照	9.1
compel	[kəmˈpel]	vt. 强迫，迫使	3.2
complaint	[kəmˈpleɪnt]	n. 抱怨	6.2

(续)

英文含义	音标	中文含义	出现章节
comprise	[kəmˈpraɪz]	vt. 包括，由……组成	4.2
concentration	[ˌkɒnsnˈtreɪʃn]	n. 浓度	2.2
conclude	[kənˈkluːd]	vt. & vi. 推断（出）	6.2
conductivity	[ˌkɒndʌkˈtɪvəti]	n. 传导性，导电性	8.1
conduit	[ˈkɒndjuɪt]	n. 导管	6.1
confirm	[kənˈfɜːm]	vt. 确认	6.2
consortium	[kənˈsɔːtiəm]	n. 财团，组合，共同体	7.2
consume	[kənˈsjuːm]	vt. 消耗	5.1
consumption	[kənˈsʌmpʃn]	n. 消费，消耗	5.1
contamination	[kənˌtæmɪˈneɪʃn]	n. 污染	9.1
continuity	[ˌkɒntɪˈnjuːəti]	n. 连续性，连通	6.1
converter	[kənˈvɜːtə(r)]	n. 变换器，变压器	1.3
convey	[kənˈveɪ]	vt. 传达，传送	2.3
coordinate	[kəʊˈɔːdɪneɪt]	vi. 协调	5.3
corrode	[kəˈrəʊd]	vt. & vi. 腐蚀，侵蚀	2.2
corrosion	[kəˈrəʊʒn]	n. 腐蚀，侵蚀	8.1
crank	[kræŋk]	vt. 起动	6.2
criteria	[kraɪˈtɪərɪə]	n. 标准，准则	7.2
crosswind	[ˈkrɒswɪnd]	n. 侧风	5.3
cylinder	[ˈsɪlɪndə(r)]	n. 圆筒，气缸	5.3
cylindrical	[səˈlɪndrɪkl]	adj. 圆柱形的	2.2
deactivation	[diːˌæktɪˈveɪʃən]	n. 失活，钝化	3.2
decelerate	[ˌdiːˈseləreɪt]	vt. & vi. （使）减速	4.2
decline	[dɪˈklaɪn]	n. 下降，衰退	1.1
decomposition	[ˌdiːkɒmpəˈzɪʃn]	n. 分解	1.2
decouple	[diˈkʌpl]	vt. 分离，解耦	5.3
defective	[dɪˈfektɪv]	adj. 有缺陷的，有瑕疵的	2.5
definition	[ˌdefɪˈnɪʃn]	n. 定义	2.1
degradation	[ˌdegrəˈdeɪʃn]	n. 恶化	2.1
degrade	[dɪˈgreɪd]	vt. 降低	2.4
deplete	[dɪˈpliːt]	vt. & vi. 耗尽，用尽	1.3
deploy	[dɪˈplɔɪ]	vt. & vi. 使展开，有效地利用	1.3
depower		vt. 断电	2.5

(续)

英文含义	音标	中文含义	出现章节
derive	[dɪˈraɪv]	vt. & vi. 源于，来自	8.2
describe	[disˈkraib]	v. 描写，叙述	2.2
diagnose	[ˈdaɪəgnəʊz]	vt. 诊断，判断	3.4
diagram	[ˈdaɪəgræm]	n. 图表，图解，示意图	8.1
differential	[ˌdɪfəˈrenʃl]	n. 差速器	4.2
diffuse	[dɪˈfjuːs]	vi. 传播，分散	8.1
disable	[disˈeɪbl]	vt. 使无能力，使残废	2.5
discharge	[disˈtʃɑːdʒ]	vt. 放电，卸船	2.1
disengagement	[ˈdɪsɪnˈgeɪdʒmənt]	n. 脱离，分离	5.3
downhill	[ˌdaʊnˈhɪl]	adv. 向下，如下坡一般	4.2
drag	[dræg]	vt. 拖拽，吃力地往前拉；n. 拖，拉，阻力	4.2
drastically	[ˈdrɑːstɪklɪ]	adv. 大幅地	5.2
durability	[ˌdjʊərəˈbɪlətɪ]	n. 耐久性，持久性	8.1
elaborate	[ɪˈlæbərət]	adj. 复杂的	2.4
electrified	[ɪˈlektrɪfaɪd]	adj. 电气化的	1.1
electrochemical	[ɪˌlektrəʊˈkemɪkəl]	adj. 电化学的	1.2
electrocute	[ɪˈlektrəkjuːt]	vt. 触电致死	6.1
electrode	[ɪˈlektrəʊd]	n. 电极	2.1
electrolyte	[ɪˈlektrəlaɪt]	n. 电解液，电解质	2.1
electromagnet	[ɪˈlektrəʊmægnət]	n. 电磁体，电磁铁	3.2
emerging	[iˈmɜːdʒɪŋ]	adj. 新兴的	2.4
emitter	[ɪˈmɪtə]	n. 发射极	3.3
employ	[ɪmˈplɔɪ]	vt. 雇用，使用，利用	1.3
energize	[ˈenədʒaɪz]	vt. 给……加电压，通电，励磁	3.2
equation	[ɪˈkweɪʒn]	n. 方程式，等式	2.2
equivalent	[ɪˈkwɪvələnt]	adj. 相当的，等效的	5.1
estimate	[ˈestɪmət]	n. & vt. 估计，估算	5.3
excitation	[ˌeksaɪˈteɪʃən]	n. 励磁	3.1
exclusively	[ɪkˈskluːsɪvlɪ]	adv. 唯一	5.3
explanation	[ˌekspləˈneɪʃn]	n. 解释，说明	7.3
exploit	[ɪkˈsplɔɪt]	vt. 开采，利用	4.2
extinguish	[ɪkˈstɪŋgwɪʃ]	vt. 熄灭（火）	2.5

(续)

英文含义	音标	中文含义	出现章节
extract	[ˈekstrækt]	v. 提取，提炼	5.3
facilitate	[fəˈsɪlɪteɪt]	vt. 促进，助长，帮助	1.3
fail-safe	[feɪl seɪf]	n. & adj. 故障安全（的），失效保护	6.2
fancy	[ˈfænsi]	adj. 精致的，豪华的	1.1
fastener	[ˈfɑːsnə(r)]	n. 紧固件	2.5
fatigue	[fəˈtiːg]	n. 疲劳，疲乏	9.2
fossil	[ˈfɒsl]	adj. 化石的，陈腐的	9.1
fouling	[ˈfaʊlɪŋ]	n. 污垢	9.1
frequent	[ˈfriːkwənt]	adj. 频繁的	1.3
fuel	[ˈfjuːəl]	n. 燃料；vt. 给……加燃料；vi. 补充燃料	1.3
full-size	[ˈfʊlˈsaɪz]	adj. 正常尺寸的，全尺寸的	5.2
gasoline	[ˈɡæsəliːn]	n. 汽油	1.3
gastight	[ˈɡæstaɪt]	adj. 不漏气的，气密	9.2
gather	[ˈɡæðə(r)]	vt. 收集	2.3
gauging	[ˈɡeɪdʒɪŋ]	n. 测量［试］，测定	2.1
graphite	[ˈɡræfaɪt]	n. 石墨	2.2
grid	[ɡrɪd]	n. 格子，格栅，管网，电网	1.3
guideline	[ˈɡaɪdlaɪn]	n. 指导方针，指导原则	7.2
gyro-accumulator	[ˌdʒaɪrəʊ-əˈkjuːmjəleɪtə(r)]	n. 陀螺蓄能器	2.1
harsh	[hɑːʃ]	adj. 严格的，残酷的	7.2
headache	[ˈhedeɪk]	n. 头痛，令人头痛的事	1.2
hit	[hɪt]	vt. 达到	5.2
hull	[hʌl]	n. 外壳，船壳，船体	7.1
humidifier	[hjuːˈmɪdɪfaɪə(r)]	n. 增湿器，加湿器	8.1
humidity	[hjuːˈmɪdəti]	n. 湿度	8.1
hybrid	[ˈhaɪbrɪd]	n. 杂交生成的生物体，混合物	1.1
hybridization	[ˌhaɪbrɪdaɪˈzeɪʃn]	n. 杂交，杂种培植，配种，杂化	4.1
hydrocarbon	[ˌhaɪdrəˈkɑːbən]	n. 碳氢化合物，烃	1.2
hydrogen	[ˈhaɪdrədʒən]	n. 氢	1.2
illustration	[ˌɪləˈstreɪʃn]	n. 说明，插图	3.2
implement	[ˈɪmplɪment]	vt. 实施，执行，实现	4.2
incorporate	[ɪnˈkɔːpəreɪt]	vi. 包含，合并，混合	5.1

(续)

英文含义	音标	中文含义	出现章节
indicate	[ˈɪndɪkeɪt]	vt. 指示，表明	3.4
indicator	[ˈɪndɪkeɪtə(r)]	n. 指示器，指标，指示灯	2.1
inexhaustible	[ˌɪnɪɡˈzɔːstəbl]	adj. 无穷无尽的，用不完的	1.2
infancy	[ˈɪnfənsi]	n. 婴儿期，摇篮时代，初期	1.3
infotainment	[ˌɪnfəʊˈteɪnmənt]	n. 信息娱乐片	5.3
infrastructure	[ˈɪnfrəstrʌktʃə(r)]	n. 基础设施；基础建设	1.2
initiation	[ɪˌnɪʃiˈeɪʃn]	n. 开始	1.1
innovative	[ˈɪnəveɪtɪv]	adj. 革新的；创新的	5.3
instruction	[ɪnˈstrʌkʃn]	n. 规程，说明（书）	9.3
insufficient	[ˌɪnsəˈfɪʃnt]	adj. 不足的	6.2
intensive	[ɪnˈtensɪv]	adj. 强烈的	1.3
interior-mounted		adj. 内部安装的，内装式	3.1
intermittent	[ˌɪntəˈmɪtənt]	adj. 间歇的	3.4
interphase	[ˈɪntəfeɪz]	n. 相间的	6.2
invention	[ɪnˈvenʃən]	n. 发明	5.2
inverter	[ɪnˈvɜːtə]	n. 逆变器，变频器	1.3
invoke	[ɪnˈvəʊk]	vi. 恳求，实行	5.3
isolate	[ˈaɪsəleɪt]	vi. 隔离	5.3
kinetic	[kɪˈnetɪk]	adj. 运动的	4.2
lifespan	[ˈlaɪfspæn]	n. 寿命	7.2
life-threatening	[laɪf ˈθretnɪŋ]	adj. 威胁生命的	2.3
lifetime	[ˈlaɪftaɪm]	n. 一生，寿命	7.2
likelihood	[ˈlaɪklihʊd]	n. 可能，可能性	7.2
lineman	[ˈlaɪnmən]	n. 架线兵，线路工人，线务员	6.1
litmus	[ˈlɪtməs]	n. 石蕊	2.5
loop	[luːp]	n. 圈，环，回路	3.2
magnet	[ˈmæɡnət]	n. 磁铁，磁体	3.1
magnetic	[mæɡˈnetɪk]	adj. 有磁性的，磁性的	3.2
malfunction	[ˌmælˈfʌŋkʃn]	n. 故障，失灵	6.2
mandatory	[ˈmændətəri]	adj. 强制的	4.1
manoeuvring	[məˈnuːvərɪŋ]	n. 机动，调遣	4.2
marginally	[ˈmɑːdʒɪnəli]	adv. 在边缘，在一定程度上，勉强合格	7.2
mathematically	[ˌmæθəˈmætɪkli]	adv. 数学上地	7.3

(续)

英文含义	音标	中文含义	出现章节
mature	[mə'tʃʊə(r)]	adj. 成熟的	7.2
measure	['meʒə(r)]	n. 度量，度量单位	2.1
megaohm	['megəʊm]	n. 兆欧	6.1
megger	['megə]	n. 绝缘电阻表	6.2
membrane	['membreɪn]	n. 薄膜，隔膜	2.2
methane	['miːθeɪn]	n. 甲烷	1.2
methanol	['meθənɒl]	n. 甲醇	1.2
methodology	[ˌmeθə'dɒlədʒi]	n. 方法，方法论	5.1
metric	['metrɪk]	n. 度量标准，尺度	7.2
minivan	['mɪnivæn]	n. 微型厢式车	1.1
model	['mɒdl]	vt. 制作模型，模仿，模拟	7.3
modify	['mɒdɪfaɪ]	vi. 修改，改变，改造	7.1
module	['mɒdjuːl]	n. 模块，模组，组件	2.1
mostly	['məʊstli]	adv. 大部分，主要地，基本上	1.3
mount	[maʊnt]	vt. 安装	4.2
mover	['muːvə(r)]	n. 原动机，发动机	4.1
moving-off	['muːvɪŋɑ̃f]	n. 移离，起步	2.1
multimeter	['mʌltimiːtə]	n. 万用表	3.4
municipal	[mjuː'nɪsɪpl]	adj. 市政的	5.3
neutralize	['njuːtrəlaɪz]	vt. 中和	2.5
niche	[nɪtʃ]	n. 壁龛，合适的位置，有利可图的缺口，商机	4.1
nitrogen	['naɪtrədʒən]	n. 氮	9.1
nomenclature	[nə'menklətʃə(r)]	n. 命名	5.3
nominal	['nɒmɪnl]	adj. 名义上的，标称的	2.1
octane	['ɒkteɪn]	n. 辛烷	1.2
offset	['ɒfset]	n. 偏移，偏离，偏差	2.3
ohmmeter	['əʊmmiːtə(r)]	n. 欧姆表	6.1
onboard	[ˌɒn'bɔːd]	adj. 随车携带的，车载的	1.3
ornate	[ɔː'neɪt]	adj. 装饰华丽的	1.1
outperform	[ˌaʊtpə'fɔːm]	vt. 胜过	6.1
outsold	[ˌaʊt'səʊld]	v. 卖得比……多	1.1
overlay	[ˌəʊvə'leɪ]	v. 叠加	4.2
oxidant	['ɒksɪdənt]	n. 氧化剂	8.1

(续)

英文含义	音标	中文含义	出现章节
pack	[pæk]	n. 包裹,一组	2.1
packaging	['pækɪdʒɪŋ]	n. 包装	2.1
parameter	[pə'ræmɪtə(r)]	n. 参数,参量	2.1
participate	[pɑː'tɪsɪpeɪt]	vi. 参加	2.2
particulate	[pɑː'tɪkjələt]	n. 微粒	9.1
perpendicular	[ˌpɜːpən'dɪkjələ(r)]	adj. 垂直的,成直角的	3.2
perspective	[pə'spektɪv]	n. 观点,看法	2.2
pertain	[pə'teɪn]	vi. 有关,附属,从属	6.2
phase	[feɪz]	n. 阶段,相	4.2
phosphoric	[fɒs'fɒrɪk]	adj. 磷的,含磷的	8.1
pickup	['pɪkʌp]	n. 皮卡	1.1
pinpoint	['pɪnpɔɪnt]	adj. 详尽的	3.4
pinpoint	['pɪnpɔɪnt]	vt. 确定	6.2
platinum	['plætɪnəm]	n. 铂,白金	8.1
plentiful	['plentɪfl]	adj. 丰富的,富产的	2.2
pollutant	[pə'luːtənt]	n. 污染物	1.3
porous	['pɔːrəs]	adj. 能穿透的,多孔性的	8.1
power	['paʊə(r)]	n. 功率,动力,权力;vt. 运转	1.2
powertrain	['paʊə(r) treɪn]	n. 动力传动系	1.3
precaution	[prɪ'kɔːʃn]	n. 预防,预防措施	3.4
prescribed	[prɪ'skraɪbd]	adj. 规定的	9.3
present	['preznt]	n. 呈现	5.1
prestigious	[pre'stɪdʒəs]	adj. 受尊敬的,有声望的	5.3
prismatic	[prɪz'mætɪk]	adj. 棱镜的,棱形	2.2
proceed	[prə'siːd]	vi. 进行	2.5
promise	['prɒmɪs]	n. 许诺,希望	2.2
promising	['prɒmɪsɪŋ]	adj. 有前途的,有希望的	8.1
propulsion	[prə'pʌlʃn]	n. 推进,推进力	1.2
proton	['prəʊtɒn]	n. 质子	2.2
proximity	[prɒk'sɪməti]	n. 接近,邻近	7.1
qualified	['kwɒlɪfaɪd]	adj. 有资格的	6.1
quantify	['kwɒntɪfaɪ]	vt. 确定……的数量,量化	2.1
range	[reɪndʒ]	n. 范围,射程,续驶里程	1.1

(续)

英文含义	音标	中文含义	出现章节
rare-earth	[ˈreərˈɜːθ]	n. 稀土	3.1
rate	[reɪt]	n. 等级；vt. 定级	5.2
rectify	[ˈrektɪfaɪ]	vt. 整流	3.3
recuperate	[rɪˈkuːpəreɪt]	vi. 再生，回收，复得	4.2
recyclable	[ˌriːˈsaɪkləbl]	adj. 可循环再用的	2.2
reformer	[rɪˈfɔːmə(r)]	n. 改革者，改良者，重整炉	1.2
relevance	[ˈreləvəns]	n. 重要性，意义，相关性	7.1
remedy	[ˈremədi]	n. 治疗法，补救办法	7.2
removal	[rɪˈmuːvl]	n. 除去，移走	6.2
represent	[ˌreprɪˈzent]	vt. 表现，象征；代表	2.1
resolver	[rɪˈzɒlvə]	n. 解析器	6.2
resort	[rɪˈzɔːt]	n. 应急措施	6.2
retainer	[rɪˈteɪnə(r)]	n. 护圈，隔环	9.2
retrieve	[rɪˈtriːv]	vt. 取回，恢复	6.2
revert	[rɪˈvɜːt]	vi. 恢复	5.3
ribbon	[ˈrɪbən]	n. 带	2.2
rotor	[ˈrəʊtə(r)]	n. 转子	3.1
roughly	[ˈrʌfli]	adv. 粗略地，大体上	9.1
route	[ruːt]	vt. 通路选定，迂回	9.2
salvage	[ˈsælvɪdʒ]	n. 经加工后重新利用的废物	2.5
scale	[skeɪl]	n. 刻度	6.1
scope	[skəʊp]	n. 示波器	3.4
secure	[sɪˈkjʊə(r)]	adj. 安全的；牢固的	3.1
security	[sɪˈkjʊərəti]	n. 安全	2.1
sedan	[sɪˈdæn]	n. 轿子，（四门）轿车	1.1
separator	[ˈsepəreɪtə(r)]	n. 隔板，分离器	2.1
sheath	[ʃiːθ]	n. 护套；vt. 包	9.2
situation	[ˌsɪtʃuˈeɪʃn]	n. 情况	4.2
slip-ring		n. 集电环	3.1
smoothness	[smuːðnəs]	n. 平滑，流畅	5.3
specification	[ˌspesɪfɪˈkeɪʃn]	n. 规格	5.2
specify	[ˈspesɪfaɪ]	vt. 指定；vi. 明确提出	3.4
spike	[spaɪk]	n. 峰，尖峰，尖端	3.3

(续)

英文含义	音标	中文含义	出现章节
spill	[spɪl]	n. 溢出（物，量）	2.5
spiral	[ˈspaɪrəl]	n. 螺旋（线）；adj. 螺旋形的	2.2
spring-loaded		adj. 受弹簧力作用的	3.2
squirrel-cage	[skˈwɪrəlkˈeɪdʒ]	n. 鼠笼式	3.2
stabilize	[ˈsteɪbəlaɪz]	vt. （使）稳定	2.5
starter	[ˈstɑːtə(r)]	n. 起动机	4.2
stator	[ˈsteɪtə]	n. 定子	3.2
status	[ˈsteɪtəs]	n. 地位，情形，状态	3.4
stop-and-go		adj. 不断走走停停的	4.2
strategy	[ˈstrætədʒi]	n. 策略，战略	1.1
stress	[stres]	n. 强调，压力，应力	6.2
submultiple	[sʌbˈmʌltɪpl]	n. 约数，因数	3.2
subset	[ˈsʌbset]	n. 子集，子系统	6.2
sulphur	[ˈsʌlfə(r)]	n. 硫磺	9.1
superior	[suːˈpɪəriə(r)]	adj. 较好的，上等的	7.2
surface-mounted		adj. 安装在表面上的	3.1
swing	[swɪŋ]	n. 摆动，摆程，振幅	6.2
symptom	[ˈsɪmptəm]	n. 症状，征兆	6.2
synchronize	[ˈsɪŋkrənaɪz]	vt. 使同步	3.3
synchronous	[ˈsɪŋkrənəs]	adj. 同步的	3.1
tab	[tæb]	n. 凸舌，连接片	2.2
technique	[tekˈniːk]	n. 技巧，技能，技术	7.3
temporarily	[tempəˈrerɪli]	adv. 暂时地，临时地	4.2
terminology	[ˌtɜːmɪˈnɒlədʒi]	n. 术语	2.1
touchpad	[ˈtʌtʃpæd]	n. 触摸板	5.3
transaxle	[trænsˈæksl]	n. 变速驱动桥	4.2
transformer	[trænsˈfɔːmə(r)]	n. 变压器	3.3
transportation	[ˌtrænspɔːˈteɪʃn]	n. 运送，运输，运输工具	1.2
turbocharge	[ˈtɜːbəʊtʃɑːdʒ]	vt. 用涡轮给（发动机）增压	5.3
ultra-capacitor	[ˌʌltrə kəˈpæsɪtə(r)]	n. 超级电容器	8.2
uncouple	[ʌnˈkʌpl]	vt. 解开，分开	4.2
underbody	[ˈʌndəˌbɒdi]	n. 底部	2.4
undergo	[ˌʌndəˈɡəʊ]	v. 经历，承受	2.2

(续)

英文含义	音标	中文含义	出现章节
unidirectional	[ˌjuːnɪdɪˈrekʃənəl]	*adj.* 单向的	2.4
uniform	[ˈjuːnɪfɔːm]	*adj.* 规格一致的，始终如一的	7.2
uninterruptedly	[ˌʌnɪntəˈrʌptɪdli]	*adv.* 不间断地	2.1
unloaded	[ʌnˈləʊdɪd]	*adj.* 空载的	2.5
unprotected	[ˌʌnprəˈtektɪd]	*adj.* 无保护的	6.1
utmost	[ˈʌtməʊst]	*adj.* 极度的，最大的	7.2
verify	[ˈverɪfaɪ]	*vt.* 核实，验证，证明	6.1
vinegar	[ˈvɪnɪɡə(r)]	*n.* 醋	2.5
voltmeter	[ˈvəʊltmiːtə(r)]	*n.* 电压表	2.5
waft	[wɒft]	*vt.* 吹送，使飘荡	5.3
wheelbase	[ˈwiːlbeɪs]	*n.* 轴距	5.3
widespread	[ˈwaɪdspred]	*adj.* 分布广的，普遍的	1.1
workbench	[ˈwɜːkbentʃ]	*n.* 工作台	2.5
wrap	[ræp]	*vt.* 包；缠绕	3.2

附录 E 传统汽车结构图解

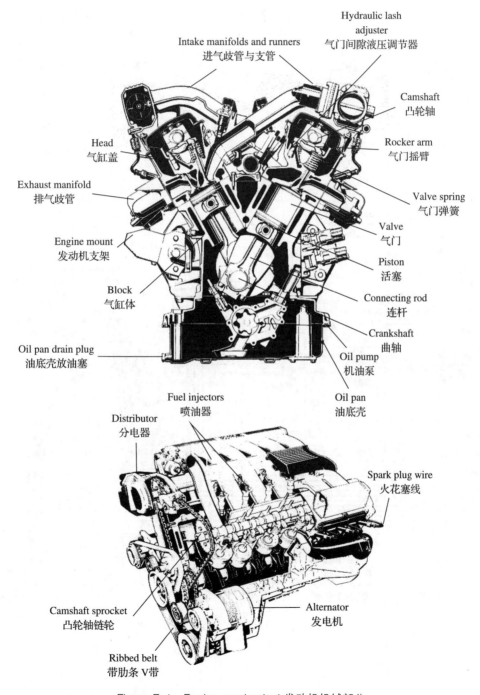

Figure E.1 Engine mechanical 发动机机械部分

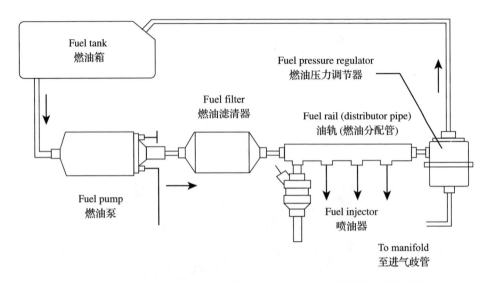

Figure E.2 Gasoline engine fuel delivery system 汽油机燃料供给系统

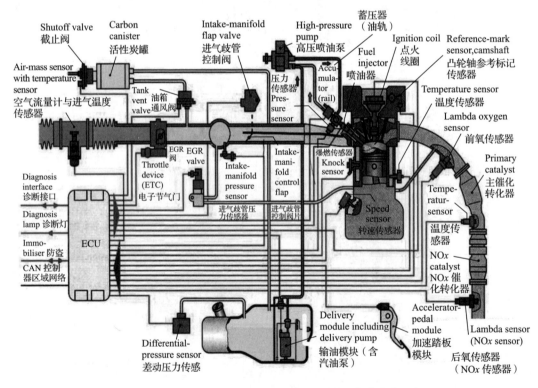

Figure E.3 Gasoline direct injection system 汽油直喷系统

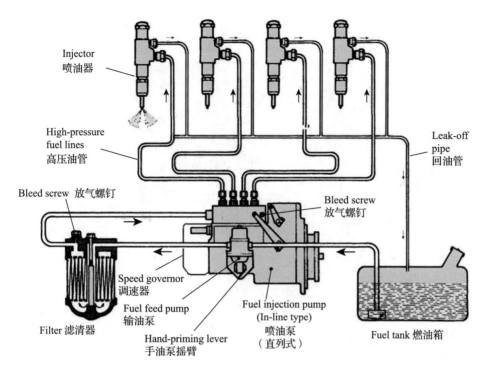

Figure E.4 Diesel fuel system 柴油机燃料系统

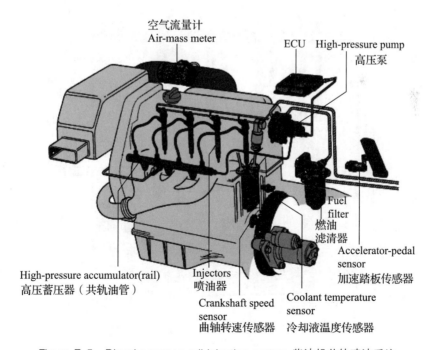

Figure E.5 Diesel common rail injection system 柴油机共轨喷油系统

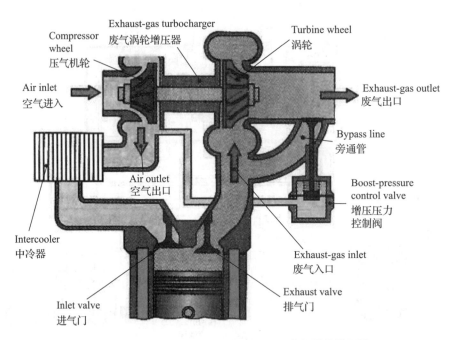

Figure E. 6　Exhaust gas turbocharger 废气涡轮增压器

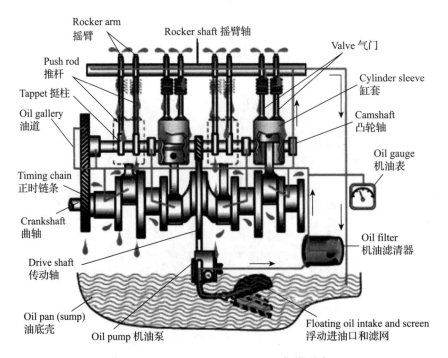

Figure E. 7　Lubrication system 润滑系统

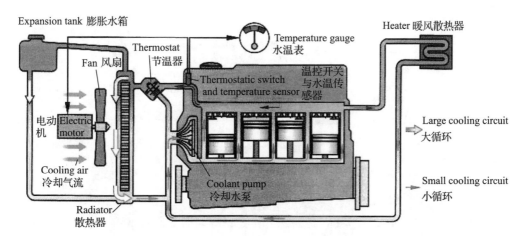

Figure E.8　Cooling system 冷却系统

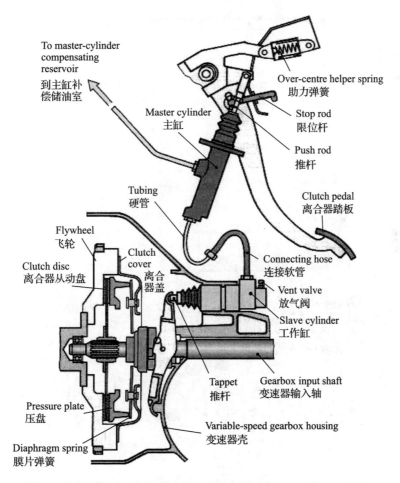

Figure E.9　Single plate clutch and its hydraulic operating system
单片离合器与液压操纵系统

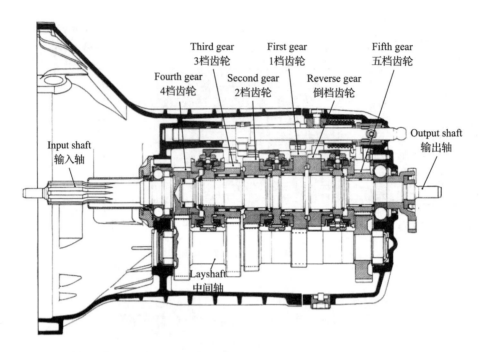

Figure E. 10　A four-speed manual transmission for rear wheel drive
用于后轮驱动的四挡手动变速器

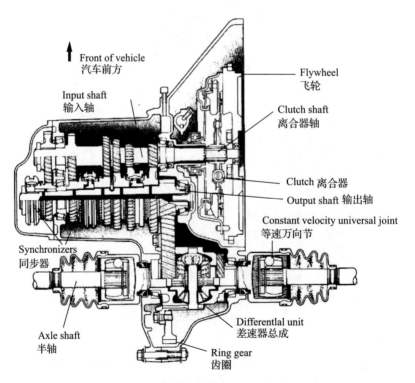

Figure E. 11　A four-speed manual transaxle for front wheel drive
用于前轮驱动的四挡手动变速驱动桥

附 录

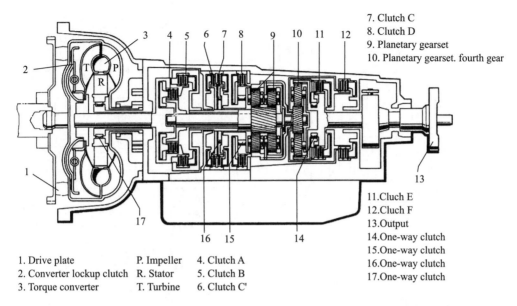

7. Clutch C
8. Clutch D
9. Planetary gearset
10. Planetary gearset. fourth gear
11. Cluch E
12. Cluch F
13. Output
14. One-way clutch
15. One-way clutch
16. One-way clutch
17. One-way clutch

1. Drive plate
2. Converter lockup clutch
3. Torque converter
P. Impeller
R. Stator
T. Turbine
4. Clutch A
5. Clutch B
6. Clutch C'

Figure E. 12　A four-speed automatic transmission 四档自动变速器

1—传动板　2—液力变矩器锁止离合器　3—液力变矩器 P—泵轮 R—导轮 T—涡轮　4—离合器 A　5—离合器 B　6—离合器 C'　7—离合器 C　8—离合器 D　9—行星齿轮组　10—行星齿轮组（四档）　11—离合器 E　12—离合器 F　13—输出轴凸缘　14—单向离合器　15—单向离合器　16—单向离合器　17—单向离合器

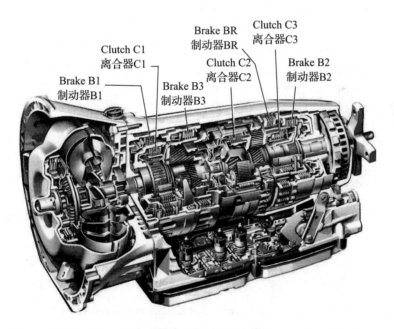

Figure E. 13　7-speed Mercedes Benz W7A 700 automatic transmission
7 档奔驰 W7A 700 型自动变速器

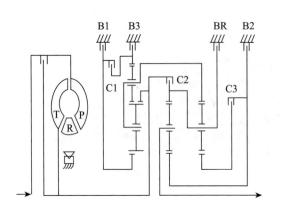

Figure E. 13　7-speed Mercedes Benz W7A 700 automatic transmission

7 档奔驰 W7A 700 型自动变速器（续）

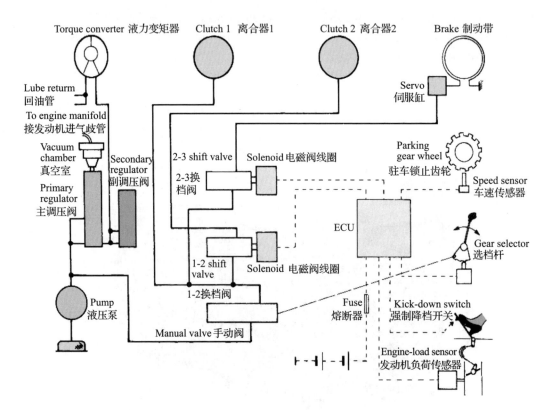

Figure E. 14　Electronically controlled automatic gearbox control system

电控自动变速器控制系统

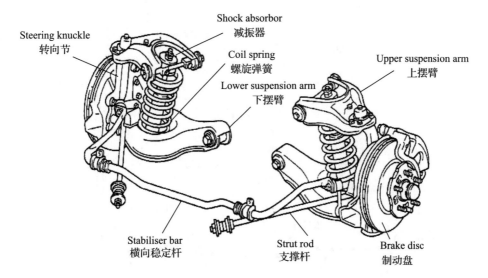

Figure E. 15 Independent front suspension 独立前悬架

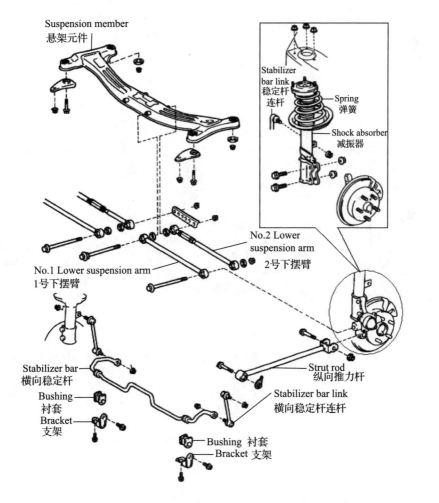

Figure E. 16 Independent rear suspension 独立后悬架

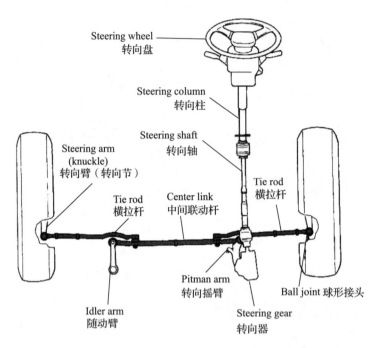

Figure E. 17　A basic steering system 一种基本的转向系统

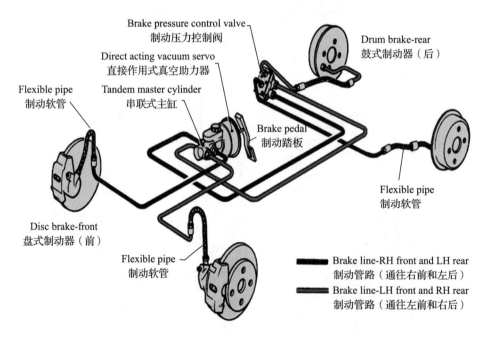

Figure E. 18　A hydraulic brake system 液压制动系统

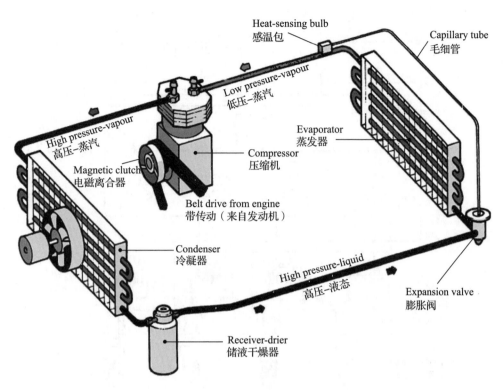

Figure E.19 A basic air conditioning system 一种基本的空调系统

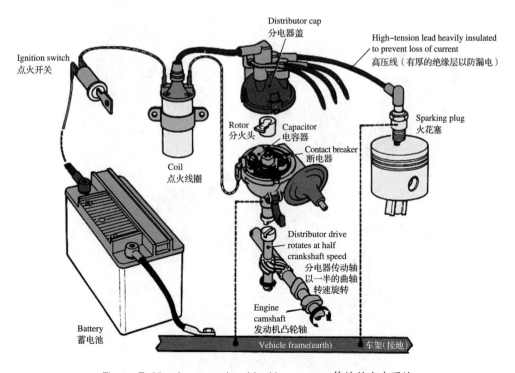

Figure E.20 A conventional ignition system 传统的点火系统

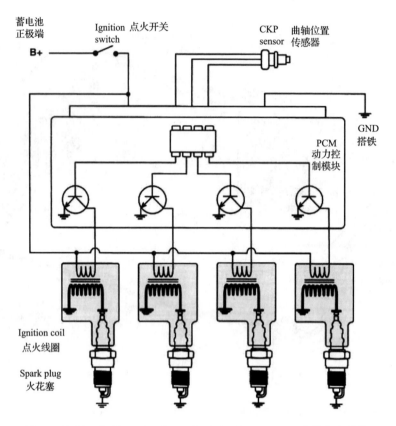

Figure E.21 A direct (coil-on-plug) ignition system 直接点火系统

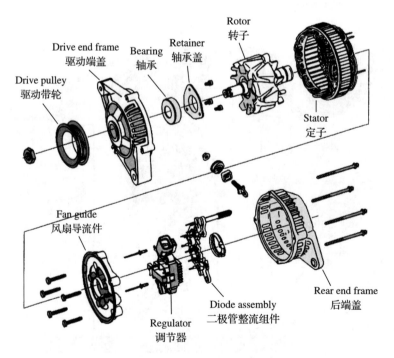

Figure E.22 Alternator 发电机

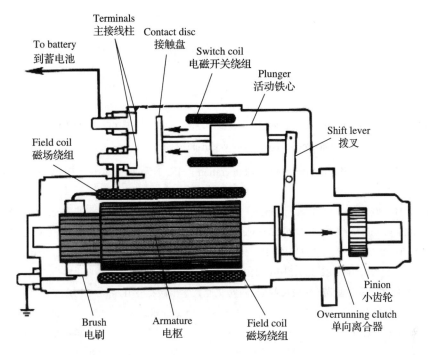

Figure E. 23　Starter motor 起动机

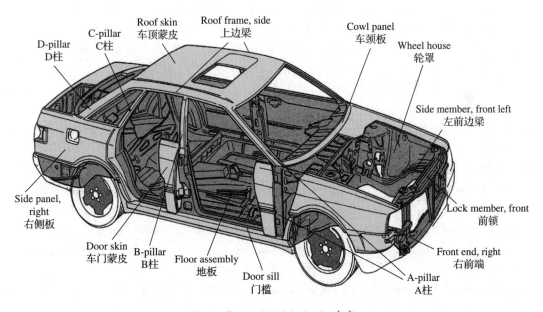

Figure E. 24　Vehicle body 车身

参 考 文 献

[1] STUART B. What we're driving: 2020 Volkswagen Passat GTE[EB/OL]. [2019-10-15] https://www.sae.org/news/2019/10/what-were-driving-volkwagen-passat-gte.

[2] İ Ş B, ALI T. Plug-in Electric Vehicle Grid Integration [M]. Norwood: Artech House, 2017:8-10, 24-27, 30-32.

[3] REESE C. The 2020 Porsche Taycan Turbo and Turbo S are here — and they're juiced[EB/OL]. https://www.autoblog.com/2019/09/04/2020-porsche-taycan-turbo-official-reveal-photos-specs/#slide-2166071.

[4] HARALD N, BERND B, JOACHIM R, et al. Automoytive transmissions [M]. 2nd ed. Heidelberg: Springer, 2011: 94,180,182-186,216-218,511-513,506.

[5] 方晓汾. 新能源汽车专业英语[M]. 西安:西安交通大学出版社,2017: 75-77,81.

[6] JAMES D, HALDERMAN. Hybrid and alternative fuel vehicles [M]. 4th ed. Hoboken: Pearson Education, Inc., 2016: 101-105, 109, 123-128, 164, 212, 214, 244, 255, 304-306,313.

[7] 麻友良,严运兵. 电动汽车概论[M]. 北京:机械工业出版社, 2012:67, 88, 157.

[8] JOSEPH A B. Modern diesel technology: electricity & electronics [M]. 2nd ed. Clifton park NY: Delmar, Cengage Learning, 2014: 239-240,246,487.

[9] The Authors of the Modern Automotive Technology Team. Modern automotive technology[M]. Haan-Gruiten: VERLAG EUROPA-LEHRMITTEL, 2006: 339,343,347,348,391,398,549-550.

[10] DAVID A C. Automotive Engineering[M]. Burlingdon: Elsevier Butterworth-Heinemann,2009: 165-167,188-191,198-200.

[11] WONG J Y. Theory of Ground Vehicles [M]. 4th ed. Hoboken, New Jersey: John Wiley & Sons, Inc., 2008: 248-251, 253.

[12] Toyota Technical Training. Toyota Hybrid system Diagnosis-Course 072[EB/OL]. http://autoshop101.com.

[13] 宋进桂. 汽车专业英语[M]. 2版. 北京:机械工业出版社, 2019:31.

[14] MARTIN W S, M T S, CHRIS J. Auto Fundamentals[M]. Tinley Park: The GOODHEART-WILLCOX COMPANY, INC., 1996: 64, 206, 347, 367, 483.

[15] Toyota Technical Training. Toyota Hybrid system-Course 071[EB/OL]. http://autoshop101.com.

[16] CALEX UK. Hillier's Fundamental of Motor Vehicle Technology [M]. 6th ed. Oxford: Oxford University Press,2014: 174, 203, 244, 263, 341, 479, 562.

[17] JAMES D H. Automotive electrical and engine performance [M]. 7th ed. Hoboken: Pearson Education, Inc., 2016:263,670-678.

[18] TONY M. 2020 Mercedes-Benz GLC 350e 4MATIC EQ Power touts bigger battery pack[EB/OL]. https://www.autoblog.com/2019/09/08/2020-mercedes-benz-glc-350e-4matic-eq-power-unveiled.